SHEILAH JANE

Shadows and Sunrises

A True Story of Shame, Strength and Rebirth Across Continents

For Mom and Dad

Contents

Preface

There were many moments when I thought I had waited too long to tell this story. Life went on, the world changed, and I wondered if it was already too late. Every time the past echoed in today—through censorship, demands for justice, or fading truth—I realized that remembering is itself a form of resistance.

I came of age under Martial Law, shaped by silence and shadows. I was taught to keep my head down, to carry on. And yet, here I am-lifting my voice, piecing together the fragments of childhood and womanhood, of shame and strength, across oceans and years.

I write now not because it is easy, but because it is necessary.

This book is not just a recounting of one life. It is a remembering. A reweaving of what was frayed by fear, by distance, by time.

It is for the girls who were once told to stay quiet. For the mothers who bore everything with grace.

For the men who labored in silence and called it love.

It is for my children, and yours, so that when they ask where we came from- they will know we rose.

There is no perfect time to speak the truth.

There is only now.

Acknowledgments

This memoir would not have been possible without so many people.

Thank you to my siblings- Jun, Bugsy and Chris- and to our mother, Lourdes. You helped fill details in my memory. More importantly, your unwavering support has helped me keep moving forward. I'm especially grateful to those who read early and later drafts, and offered thoughtful feedback, with a special nod to my sister Bugsy for her insight and encouragement.

To Todd, my life partner: thank you for your patience with the late-night edits and the endless stream of emails I sent myself in the middle of the night.

To the teachers and friends who helped shape my journey- thank you for planting seeds of knowledge, compassion, and courage along the way.

To Dan, the father of my children- thank you for being a great father, and for the life we had together.

To my niece Jerzey- thank you for capturing the spirit of this memoir so beautifully through your cover design. Your art brings the story to life. Follow her creations on Instagram: @jeiribellie.

And foremost, to my children- Mark, Rence and Danielle, my inspiration for this memoir. Everything begins and ends with you.

May this story help you understand where we've been, and guide you toward where you're meant to go.

PROLOGUE: The Promise of October

"Sometimes, silence is not weakness. It is simply the absence of the right words."
   -The author

They said I was going places.

Many of us, when we were young, were asked the same questions by family or friends: What do you want to be when you grow up? Why?

I was the girl with the top grades; the one called to the front of every school assembly. I was the dependable class officer, the one who volunteered for church events. A scholarship was waiting for me—an open door to study abroad, to dream bigger than my small hillside town. Teachers praised me. Neighbors boasted about me. My parents, despite our modest means, believed I would be the one to lift us up.

But life is never just a straight path. Not when you are young, aching to be seen, and living in a world where expectations press on you like the mountain fog—soft at first, but soon thick enough to blind.

At the time, our answers were often vague, dreamy, and ever-changing. One day, we'd dream of being an astronaut, flying through the stars.

1

The next, a teacher or an artist. Maybe even a doctor, curing diseases and saving lives. For most, the answer changed daily and was rarely a single thing.

But there was a question no one seemed to ask:

How? How would you become what you wanted to be? How would you navigate the obstacles, the unknowns, the unexpected turns? Some figure it out quickly. Others take longer. For some, the how unfolds as a straight line; for others, it twists and bends, like a river carving its way through uncharted terrain.

I was sixteen when the first twist in my river appeared. That moment at sixteen cracked something open in me- marking the beginning of a journey I never saw coming- one filled with heartbreak, resilience, sacrifice, and transformation.

At that age, the world felt limitless, brimming with possibilities. I had dreams, big ones, and a plan- or at least the start of one. I'd just been awarded an academic scholarship. It wasn't just any scholarship. It was the kind that allowed me to study at any college of my choice, not only in my country but in the USA, where opportunities seemed endless.

I was buzzing with excitement. My family's sacrifices had paid off, and I could see their pride reflected in their eyes. This wasn't just my dream- it was theirs too. We started making plans: Where would I apply? What would I major in? Geology, to travel the world? Linguistics, to work for the UN? Maybe even law- justice had always stirred something in me. Would I stay close to home and attend the University of the Philippines, or aim for the stars with applications to

NYU or Harvard?

The possibilities glittered like constellations- within sight, just out of reach.

But then, life- as it does-, took an unexpected turn.

This is the story behind the headlines, behind the whispers that once trailed me through market stalls and school corridors. It's about what was lost, and what was forged in the quiet wreckage that followed. It's about shame, yes- but also about resilience. About the moments no one saw. About the ones I held on to like lifelines. And the ones I nearly drowned in.

This is the story of how dreams evolve and how, even in the face of life's most unexpected turns, we find a way forward.

I didn't know then how deeply the world could break you. Or how strong you have to become just to keep walking.

But I know now.

And I'm still here.

Chapter 1: Of Wild Orchids and Waterfalls

"We could never have loved the earth so well if we had no childhood in it."

- George Eliot

I still remember the smell of mud and muddy water; musty, earthy like the smell of mushroom, not unpleasant but with a peculiar odor. The mud was cool and squelchy between our toes, its earthy scent mingling with the fragrance of wet rice stalks. The smell and feel of mud were more than just an earthy scent; it was the essence of my childhood.

Growing up, we were always streaked with mud- our knees caked, our hands sticky, our hair wild with wind. Our laughter echoed across the paddies as we hopped from one narrow ridge to the next, balancing like tightrope walkers, trying not to slip into the murky green water below. My younger brother Jun, always the cautious one, would assess the waters before leaping in with the rest of us. Sometimes we lost, landing with a splash and squeal, the rice stalks swaying in quiet amusement.

Afterward, we'd race each other to the nearby waterfalls, bare feet slapping against the warm earth, our limbs pumping with the last of our energy, the echo of our laughter bouncing from mountains to rocks and back. The cold mountain water would hit us like a thousand tiny needles, shocking our sun-warmed skin. We shrieked, hollered, and let it wash over us - mud, sweat, and all- until we were clean and breathless. Our clothes clung to our bodies, soaked and heavy, but we didn't care! We sprawled across the smooth boulders, our backs pressed to warm stone, eyes closed, letting the thunder of falling water fill our ears and empty our thoughts.

The fresh mountain air filled our lungs with something that felt close to joy. Mist from the falls sprayed over us, catching the sunlight and creating halos of tiny rainbows that shimmered in the air. We reached for them like treasure, wondering if there really was a pot of gold at the end. That magical stillness never lasted long. The gurgle of our stomachs reminded us that we were still just kids- and hungry ones at that. We'd leap to our feet, call out our goodbyes to the others, and skip barefoot back down the path toward home, the sun warm on our backs and the promise of dinner pulling us home.

Summers were a blur of scraped elbows, sticky mango fingers, and dusty feet. We climbed trees like monkeys, launched stones across ponds in fierce competitions, and ran wild until the light began to fade. The rice paddies weren't just fields to us- they were kingdoms and battlefields, oceans, and racetracks. They were our entire world, wide and waiting.

Of course, we didn't know then that we were playing among wonders; these weren't just ordinary fields. We were playing on sacred ground, on the legendary rice terraces of Ifugao-carved by hand into the northern mountains of the Philippines more than two thousand years ago. Generations of hands had shaped those slopes, stone by stone, creating stairways of green that clung to the mountainsides like ribbons. Just like many children before us, we ran through history without even realizing it.

The Philippines is an archipelago in Southeast Asia made up of more than 7,000 islands. It is divided into three main island groups: Luzon to the north, Visayas in the center, and Mindanao to the south. My province, Ifugao, is nestled in the Cordillera Mountain range in Luzon- rugged, forested, and rich with the legacy of our ancestors.

These rice terraces were more than a stunning landscape- they were a testament to our ancestors' genius. We thought of them as stairways to heaven, etched into the mountains, rising steeply into the clouds. Recognized by UNESCO as a World Heritage Site, these terraces have been cultivated for over two thousand years. Their vast scale and intricate design stand as a marvel of ancient engineering and endurance.

Water flowed gently through stone and mud walls, fed by an intricate network of canals that drew from forest springs and mountain streams. During the growing season from December to May, the terraces shimmered with life- lush green rice stalks swaying in the breeze, their fragrance mingling with the scent of wet earth and fresh leaves. In mid-June as harvest neared, the green faded into gold and amber, the rice heavy on its stem giving off the subtle aroma of popcorn, the surrounding foliage still vivid with the stubborn greens of the highlands.

Rice Terraces of the Philippine Cordilleras, Copyright: Patrick Venenoso

As we played in the forests, splashing in the waterfalls and running through the rice paddies, my mother always reminded us to be careful of strange men lurking in the dense jungles. I never quite understood her caution until years later when she shared a story from the past. She informed us that, during World War II, some Japanese soldiers who did not know the war had ended remained hidden in the jungles we visited. They feared being accused of desertion by the Japanese government and stayed in isolation, only appearing after another retired Japanese soldier coaxed them back into the world. A few years after my birth in 1970, a retired Japanese soldier persuaded two individuals to emerge from hiding. They were hiding in the dense jungles of the southern parts of the Philippines.

My mother's warnings stayed with me, a subtle reminder that the land we loved had its own dark history, one I was too young to understand at the time. Her warnings, I didn't realize then, were just one way that she showed her protective nature, a protective nature that would manifest many times later.

Photos of the terraces now look almost otherworldly- mist draped over ancient ridges, colors saturated by filters and drone shots. Travelers and bloggers marvel at their beauty, calling them bucket-list-worthy, posting captions like "Nature's masterpiece" or "Lost Eden."

And don't get me wrong- they are beautiful.

But back then, they were simply home.

As a child, I never thought much about the beauty of the terraces- they were just there, part of my everyday world. I barely noticed the way the morning mist curled around the mountaintops or how the golden rice stalks swayed in unison like a well-rehearsed dance.

It was where we spent countless school breaks- playing in the mud, washing clothes by hand, cooling off under waterfalls. On the way home, we'd climb trees, daring each other to reach the highest branches. One afternoon, I scrambled up a guava tree with the fearless confidence of a child who thought she might be part monkey. The branch I chose wasn't that high- just enough to make me feel invincible.

Then I heard it: a sharp, splintering crack.

Before I could react, the branch gave way. For a heartbeat, I was suspended midair- weightless- then came the plunge. I hit the ground hard, the wind knocked clean from my lungs. Stunned, I lay there blinking at the sky, trying to remember how to breathe.

Then, with a dull thud, the branch landed after me.

I squeezed my eyes shut, bracing for pain- but instead, something strange. The branch didn't slam flat against me. It curved naturally, arching over me like a bent elbow. I was trapped beneath it, but completely unharmed.

For a few seconds, I just lay there, dazed. If the straight part had hit me, it could have meant broken ribs- or worse. But luck, or maybe the forest itself, had spared me.

As soon as I could move, my siblings and friends burst into laughter. They yanked the branch off me, still giggling. "You looked like a bug stuck under a leaf!" someone said. I forced a shaky laugh, brushing dirt from my arms and pretending I wasn't rattled.

We kept climbing trees after that. But I never sat on a branch the same way again. Even as a child, the near-miss moment felt like a gentle warning of what could happen if I didn't learn from it.

Once you've fallen, you learn to respect the heights you used to take for granted. But this fall was nothing compared to what was to come.

Amidst our adventures in the forests, we'd also pick wild orchids from tree trunks for my mother. She would say, "These are beautiful, thank you!" even when they probably weren't. But she loved orchids, and her face lit up every time we brought her a new bouquet, which she would graft on tree trunks, bringing the wild, exotic beauty of the forest to our home. She removed dead leaves and wilted flowers but otherwise left them alone. "They are wildflowers, so they do not need a lot of attention. Mother nature would take care of them here, as she did in the forest," she once said. I shrugged and walked away, having understood what she said but not quite what she meant. It would be many years later before that metaphor sunk in. I didn't realize then that she was describing us too.

We were wildflowers in our own right- tough, untamed, and growing in the cracks of a world that didn't make room for softness. My mother never said it outright, but I think she believed that if we could thrive under the harshest sun, we'd survive anything.

We weren't just having fun; we also had responsibilities. One of the many chores my siblings and I had was fetching water. Because we didn't have indoor plumbing, we needed to fill pails of water to bring to the house. Those can be heavy, and the handles were not comfortable, they would leave marks on our hands.

Due to the mountainous terrain of where we lived, the water table was lower than where the house was. So, unlike Jack & Jill in the nursery rhyme, we went down the hill to fetch water, then we lumbered up with our pails full of water. Once or twice, one of us would slip and tumble down the hill. Luckily, no one ever broke their arm.

Often, we wouldn't bother searching and just called out, "Mom, we can't find the pails!" To which she would always answer, "Use your eyes, not your mouth!" We would roll our eyes, look for the pails and fetch water.

Fetching water was a daily ritual that taught us the value of hard work. The pails were heavy, and the journey uphill left our arms aching, but the sense of accomplishment as we filled the large clay jars and aluminum basins back home was unmatched.

Even so, at that time it was my least favorite chore! Then again, I didn't have a favorite chore! Like any kid, I loved to play. Sometimes I would complain about having to do my assigned chores, whether it's sweeping the floor, washing the dishes or babysitting my younger siblings, but I did them anyway, grudgingly. They were assigned to me so no one else would do them. When chores piled up and my mother was busy, she sometimes hired help, but usually we did them ourselves.

But even amidst our obligations, there were lessons waiting in the soil. I used to groan whenever my mother pulled me away from playing to help her in the garden. My hands ached from pulling weeds, my back sore from bending over. I didn't understand why she cared so much about every little plant, why she hummed to them as if they could hear her. Now, years later, the rare moments that I find myself kneeling in my own garden, my fingers sifting through soil, I remember the quiet rhythm of her hands. Maybe that was her lesson all along- that beauty and strength often bloom where we least expect them.

Life in the mountains wasn't just about work or play-it was also about celebration. There were always parties, whether for baptisms, weddings, or even funerals. One of my favorites is the festival after the harvest. The men of the village would do the traditional tug-of-war, and the winning group was believed to have a bountiful harvest the next season. During the harvest festivals, the elders would gather us around the fire, their voices weaving tales of ancient heroes and mythical creatures that once roamed our land. These stories were not just entertainment; they were lessons in courage, honor, and respect for the earth. They would tell us stories of how our people came to be, about the first man and woman to inhabit our province, and how they instilled in us our heritage.

The Bugan and Wigan story is a traditional Ifugao myth, where they are considered the first man and woman. They are said to be the children of the supreme deity, the sky god, Kabunyan, who sent them down to Earth to populate it. The story often revolves around their role in setting up the rice cultivation practices that are central to Ifugao culture. It also highlights the responsibility of the Ifugao people to care for their land and cultivate rice properly.

As a young child, I was a bit confused about the Bugan and Wigan story. I was also in Sunday school learning about Adam and Eve so I would wonder if there were two worlds, each with their own first man and woman, and I just happened to live where Bugan and Wigan lived. And the other world was someplace else- maybe another planet. Some years after that, I came to understand the situation. These stories that run parallel with each other is our way of connecting to the past to understand the present, and it doesn't matter whether it was folklore or scripture. What matters is not just whether they are true or not, but how they help us to remember who we are.

The elders also told us amidst the hiss of a cooking fire or the crackle of burning bonfire wood that we must give thanks for what we have, or the gods will take them away. These stories were repeated each time there was a gathering, so they stayed with us. But as children then, we would nod our heads like we understood, but our minds were elsewhere, we were thinking of joining the fun happening around us. At that time, we were only half listening- but now I realize those myths were anchoring us in something much larger.

These blending of worlds- spiritual, ancestral and lived- was part of our everyday rhythm. Whether we were singing hymns in Sunday School or watching elders perform rituals during planting season, it all seemed to belong to one story we were still learning to understand.

These gatherings were loud and lively, with music and dancing. Music was produced with traditional hand-held smooth surfaced and narrow rimmed bronze gongs called gangha. The gangha can be played in various styles, including toppaya (played on the lap) and pattung (suspended from the hand and played with a stick). A set of gangha typically consists of multiple gongs, each tuned to different notes. The dancing is called Dinuyya. Central to the Dinuyya is the eagle, a symbol of strength, freedom, and vision in the Ifugao culture.

The men wore their traditional wanoh – a type of loincloth, specific to the Ifugao culture in the Philippines. It's known for its specific design and weaving techniques, often featuring a central stripe with human figures and other intricate patterns. The women wore their tolgè or tapis- the traditional clothing for Ifugao women that typically includes a wraparound skirt, and a blouse called a lamma. The tolge can have various designs and colors depending on the specific region and clan. The lamma, originally used for sun protection, has evolved into a more ornate blouse with stitches, patterns, and even sleeves.

Male and female dancers move like eagles, extending their arms like wings to honor their warrior ancestors' bravery. This dance is not just a victory dance: it also plays a role in Ifugao courtship and marriage. The beat always gave me a feeling of joy, of elation, soaring, with no care in the world.

Then there are the endless plates of food. Families of higher stature in the community would butcher a cow, while others served pork, and the whole town is invited. More often than not, the next town over is also in attendance. No matter what the occasion, there was always rice wine brewed by a family member.

The rice wine in my province is called baya. It's a fermented rice wine made from glutinous rice and a native herb called onwad, a woody herb that acts as a yeast agent. After fermentation, the wine is transferred from the large clay vessels to jugs, leaving the mash in the vessels. Of course, my young friends and I were not allowed to partake of the wine so we would sneak out handfuls of the mash and laughed as we devoured them, delighting in something forbidden. Sometimes we would get caught, "Put that back!" We would hear an adult yell, and we were forced to return the mash. Getting caught was part of the fun, so it didn't dissuade us from trying to sneak out mash whenever we could. We loved eating the leftover mash- it was soft, like regular cooked rice, but it was sticky and sweet but not overly sweet, and sometimes it made us a little dizzy from the residual alcohol!

We didn't celebrate Halloween back then- though now we do just like the rest of the world- but November 1st- All Saints' Day, or the Day of the Dead- was a holiday of its own kind. We cleaned gravesites, adorned them with flowers, and gathered as a family to share food and stories about the loved ones who passed away. One of the relatives would inevitably play the guitar, and we'd sing along, voices echoing under the starlit sky. If we stayed late enough, someone always lit a bonfire. It was both a fun and loving way to commemorate our departed. For us, even death was met with warmth and music.

Going to these celebrations can be a trek sometimes. Getting around our mountainous town wasn't always easy. We didn't have a car, so most of the time, we piled into jeepneys, the colorful public utility vehicles that were as much a cultural icon as they were transportation. Painted with bright patterns, slogans, and sometimes religious imagery, Jeepneys were always lively. I remember hanging off the sides when the seats were full, laughing as the Jeepney rumbled along dirt roads. They felt like an extension of the community-inventive, chaotic, vibrant, and always moving forward.

Their inventiveness and vibrancy were in the fact that they transformed US military jeeps left behind after World War II. Local mechanics converted the jeeps into buses with galvanized or stainless-steel bodies, to what is now jeepneys.

Sometimes we would race downhill with these jeepneys in our home-made bobsleds. Our uncles would fashion these bobsleds made of plywood as the floorboard, tree branches for steering wheels and footrests, and another piece of wood tied to the floorboard as hand brakes. We would squeal as we went downhill- our hearts racing and our palms scraped- as we held on to our wooden brakes sending out sparks as we made sure we steered towards the hillside as we went down the bottom of the road. The drivers would scream at us, "Get out of the road. You're going to get hurt!" We would just jump up and down and cheer as the jeepneys roared past us.

We loved racing down any hill! Riding on Betel Nut palm tree leaves we call Opak, or a piece of cardboard down a muddy hill felt like the most important thing in the world back then. We whooped and hollered, crashing into each other like wild things. I didn't realize what truly mattered wasn't the ride itself, but the laughter we shared, the way we cheered each other on, and how, for those few moments, we felt invincible.

But our pants were not. We would end up with holes on the cheeks of our pants.

"Stop ruining your pants. You'll end up with patches on the butt part!" Our mother would scold us, as she sewed the patches using the zigzag feature of her beloved sewing machine. Then it became a competition- who would end up with patches on both butt cheeks?

She pretended to be stern, but sometimes I caught her shaking her head, hiding a smile. Her exasperation was always stitched through with affection, just like those patches.

My sister Bugsy, with her mischievous grin, was always my partner in crime during our escapades. If only life let us hold onto that feeling a little longer. We were so young, and adventurous. I smile whenever I think of this. My siblings and I still talk about our childhood adventures! It's amazing how none of us were seriously hurt. We got away with minor knee and elbow scratches.

We were always outdoors, walking everywhere - school, the market, church. It could be exhausting, especially under the sweltering sun. Sometimes we'd complain to our mother about being tired. She'd let us rest a little, then gently nudge us forward again. We didn't stay inside much, except during the wet season.

In the Philippines, there are only two seasons: wet-hot or dry-hot.

You know the saying, "When it rains, it pours?" Well, in our case, it didn't just pour- it came down in torrents, and sometimes sideways. An umbrella was practically useless. I remember trying to hold it over my head, then to one side, then over my head again- and still ending up

16

drenched. Sometimes the rain would last for days. We'd grow restless, itching to go back outside.

We didn't have a television at home, but that didn't stop us from wanting to watch one. Every so often, my siblings and I would plead with our mother: "Can we go to the neighbor's house to watch TV?"

She would sigh, pretending to consider it, though we already knew the answer.

"You have one hour," she'd say, holding up a single finger for emphasis. "And no soap operas! Those are illusions- they are not real life."

At the time, her words meant little to us. We were too young to grasp what she meant by "illusions of life." All we knew was that those soap operas had beautiful people with dramatic lives, whispering secrets or crying over betrayals. But we weren't there for the drama- we just wanted to watch something, anything, that flickered on that magical screen.

We would race to our neighbor's house, squeeze onto their wooden benches, and stare, wide-eyed, at the glowing box. Whether it was a variety show, a cartoon, or even the evening news, it didn't matter. It felt like stepping into another world.

True to our promise, we always returned home after an hour. My mother never asked what we had watched- she only reminded us, repeatedly, that television wasn't real life. "Stories are stories," she'd say, "but don't get lost in them."

It took me years to understand what she meant. Looking back now, I think she was teaching us to live in the real world- not in the fantasies on a screen. But at the time, we just nodded, shrugged, and waited for the next chance to visit the neighbor's house.

On rainy days when we couldn't play outside, we turned to board games to pass the time. Chess, Scrabble, and a few well-worn decks of playing cards became our entertainment. I remember sitting cross-legged on the floor, my siblings and I hunched over the wooden chessboard, deep in thought, strategizing our next move. Scrabble matches would turn into heated battles, each of us scrambling to form the longest or most complex word we could muster.

I didn't know it at the time, but those rainy days spent poring over letters and words planted a love for word games that has stayed with me to this day. Now, I can spend hours playing Quordle and Words with Friends, testing my vocabulary just as I did as a child. My friends often groan when I win, laughing as they say, 'Oh, I hate you!' But I just smile- it all started with those rainy afternoons, a Scrabble board, and a house full of restless kids looking for fun.

Growing up with limited resources wasn't easy, but I never felt lacking. Life was simple, yet every moment was rich. My community's resilience became my own, a foundation I've carried with me ever since. From the terraces that touched the sky to the muddy games in the paddies, everything was woven with joy, family, and tradition. Little did I know, those carefree days in the rice terraces would soon be replaced by challenges that tested my strength in ways I could never have imagined. These terraces embody the resilience and ingenuity of my people- a resilience that calls to me, urging me to face life's challenges with the same unwavering spirit.

Looking back, I see the magic in it all. Those early years feel like a blur of wild orchids and waterfalls- moments of quiet beauty nestled among the chaos of muddy shoes, skinned knees, and the scent of woodsmoke. I didn't yet have the words for what I was learning, but I felt it: not just in the beauty of the terraces or the joy of childhood games, but in the lessons of perseverance, gratitude, and belonging, in my mother's steady voice, in the rhythms of the land, in the hush that followed a storm. Life was not always easy, but it was full. That childhood, shaped by the land, the culture, and the people who made it home, is still my greatest treasure- and somehow, that treasure would carry me forward, like water finding its way down the mountain.

But beyond the terraces and waterfalls were the messier unknown truths of family life- the small miracles and daily mischiefs that shaped us more than we realized.

Chapter 2: Mud, Mischief and Miracles

"We do not remember days, we remember moments."
-Cesare Pavese

I am the firstborn of four children: myself, Jun who is two years my junior, Bugsy two years Jun's junior, then Chris. But I grew up surrounded by a sprawling extended family. My mother was the second of twelve children, and my father was the second of five. Life was always full, chaotic, and colorful. Even as a child, I knew we didn't have much. My parents, fresh out of college, started their careers as substitute schoolteachers- a common path for new graduates in our town. This meant moving wherever the Provincial Department of Education found them work.

Each new town came with temporary housing: the Teachers' Quarters. These weren't houses as much as shared living spaces, with one or two bedrooms assigned per family. The living room and kitchen were communal, and indoor plumbing was a luxury we didn't have. The "bathroom" was a small wooden structure standing alone in the backyard. Inside, the scent of damp earth mixed with the fresh scent of soap and shampoo. Outside, insects buzzed lazily in the dim light filtering through the gaps in the wooden walls. A large tub of cold water sat nearby for bathing. We had electricity but the rolling black outs made it unreliable. So more often than not, we heated water by boiling it over a wood fire, the smoky scent clinging to our clothes and hair. When the water was hot, we poured it into the tub and used a small plastic bucket with a handle- our beloved tabo, or what we later joked was our "bathtub-o"- to scoop and pour the water over ourselves. The toilet? It was an outhouse. Just a deep hole in the ground, replaced with another hole when the first one filled up.

I remember the clang of shared pots in the kitchen, kids from other families darting in and out of rooms like it was one giant house. There were squabbles over who got to stir the pot of rice, and quiet alliances formed over stolen mango slices.

The kitchen was another challenge. Gas was expensive, so most of the time, we cooked with firewood. During the dry season, the wood was left outside to bake under the sun, its scent earthy and sharp. But during the rainy months, damp logs stubbornly refused to light. We stacked them on a wire rack above the wood stove, hoping the rising heat would dry them enough for use. When they were not dry enough, the fire would sputter and crackle before belching thick, suffocating smoke that filled the entire house. The acrid burn of it stung our eyes and scratched at our throats, forcing us to fling open every door and window. Sometimes, the smoke was so thick we had to run outside, gasping for fresh air, our faces streaked with soot. Nowadays, this would be a fire code violation! Despite the smoke and soot, the aroma of our traditional dishes like sinigang and adobo filled our home, a comforting reminder of our heritage.

But back then, I never questioned any of it. I thought that's just how life was.

The specifics of all the places we lived blur together now, except for a couple.

You might have already guessed that my siblings and I loved being outdoors. A little bit of rain didn't bother us either, and that tendency got my brother Jun and me into more than our fair share of trouble.

I do not remember the exact town we were living in at the time, only that we were renting an apartment instead of staying in the Teachers' Quarters. That alone was a luxury. The apartment had better accommodations, and most importantly, we had a first-floor unit. By that time, our little sister Bugsy was an infant. Bugsy is a nickname she got years later. It also happens to fit as a spunky version of her native name, Bugan. In our culture, each newly born child inherits a native name after an elder in the family, whether it is a grandparent or a great-grandparent. The native name is not included in the birth certificate; only Christian names are registered. How the Christian names were chosen was random. But the native name is respected and acknowledged by the community.

Among the elders, to be named after an ancestor was to carry their virtues and burdens. It was a silent expectation, passed down like a whispered prayer. Bugsy never shrugged that off- she embraced it like a challenge.

My siblings and I each have a native name, but Bugsy's has the best backstory of all. Bugan is not only the name of our maternal great-grandmother, but also the name of the first woman to inhabit our province- our Eve. When we were in college and the movie Bugsy, about gangster Bugsy Siegel, came out in theaters. My sister decided to trade Bugan for Bugsy, and it has been her nickname ever since.

She more than lived up to it. Small and short though she may be, she made it to the Saint Louis University varsity women's basketball team. She had the sweetest layup I have ever seen- smooth, quick, effortless. She could maneuver and weave her way beneath the taller players like she belonged in the gaps. Whoosh!

"She may be little, but she is fierce," her teammates used to say.

Off the court, Bugsy moved with the same quiet precision- only instead of weaving past defenders, she wove through the tension in our family. She became our soft translator, the one who buffered my fire with her calm, who carried messages across emotional borders like peace offerings. Where I could be sharp, she smoothed the edges. Like our mother, she didn't raise her voice to be heard- she simply listened until others quieted down.

Our days in that tiny apartment were full of tiny adventures. From the window of our new apartment, Jun and I watched the rain pour down in thick sheets, the scent of wet earth and concrete drifting in.

"Can we go outside and play?" we begged our mother. "The rain isn't that strong."

"No," she muttered, barely looking up. "You'll get your clothes covered in mud again."

But we were persistent. We asked again. And again. And again.

She kept refusing, so when she stepped into the bedroom to put Bugsy down for a nap, we made our move. We tiptoed to the door, then dashed outside, the cool rain soaking through our clothes in seconds.

We laughed, shrieking as we splashed in puddles, our feet squelching in the mud. We were soaked to the skin and shivering in minutes, but we were thrilled. The world felt fresh and wild, and for those brief moments, we were untouchable. It was glorious!

Then the door slammed open, and we heard her.

"Get inside! Now!"

Her voice cut through the rain, sharp as a whip. We turned and saw her standing at the door, arms crossed, eyes blazing. Our victory was short-lived.

We trudged in, trailing muddy water like guilty little snails, we slunk inside, still giggling- until she marched over and stripped us of our wet, muddy clothes.

"You want to play in the rain? Fine. But you will do it naked next time."

The horror of the idea silenced us at once. We sat there, shivering and mortified, our laughter completely gone.

"I don't want to go outside naked," I whispered to Jun.

He shook his head, eyes wide. Jun and I glanced at each other, a flicker of shared regret and amusement passing between us. We were co-conspirators again, bound not by blood but the thrill of rebellion and the chill of consequence. Lesson learned. We never did that again.

Years later, Jun and I laughed about that moment, but even now, when the sky darkens and the thunder rolls in, I feel a flicker of that childhood thrill- and the weight of my mother's love, fierce and unrelenting, like the rain itself.

That wasn't the last time Jun, and I got into mischief, but nothing- not scraped knees or scoldings- could have prepared us for what happened next.

I was about six years old and in first grade. Dad was leaving early for his office in the next province, while the school grounds bustled with activity. It was the Annual Zonal Meet, and the air buzzed with excitement. The field was alive with the pounding of feet, the shouts of players, and the shrill blasts of whistles. Jun, only four at the time, and I ran freely through the crowd, swept up in the joy of the day. My sister Bugsy, still a toddler, clung to my mother's skirt as she sat on the sidelines, chatting with other parents. My mother was five months pregnant with our youngest brother at the time, so she was taking it easy.

Then everything changed.

I heard my mother scream.

Not the irritated, I'm scolding-you kind of scream. This was different- raw, panicked. I had never heard anything like it. I turned to see her sprinting across the field, her face pale with terror.

Confused, I chased after her, my small legs struggling to keep up.

She stopped abruptly, dropped to her knees, and let out a wail I will never forget.

Just a few steps behind her, I froze.

There on the ground lay my little brother. A javelin lay beside him. His guts were spilling out of his punctured stomach.

The world tilted. The field, once so full of life and laughter, blurred into a nightmarish haze.

What happened next is a fog of frantic voices and motion. My mother used her bare hands to push Jun's intestines back into his stomach while calling out to one of the nearby mothers for something- anything- to wrap around his tiny body.

There were no ambulances. No paramedics. This was in a remote town in the 1970s Philippines. The school was nestled down a hill from the highway, surrounded by rice fields. My mother quickly left instructions with the women to look after Bugsy, while a Good Samaritan carried Jun up the hill through the paddies. My mother and I followed, running up the hill as fast as my feet could carry me. One of my slippers got stuck on the tall grass. I bent down to retrieve it, but my mother pulled me up before I could. There was no time.

At the top, a construction crew resting by the roadside saw us. One of the workers offered to drive us to the town hospital in his dump truck.

When we arrived, there was no surgeon, so the attending physician administered anesthesia, and we immediately set off again- still in the same dump truck- for the provincial hospital, about an hour and a half away.

Bundled up, Jun lay quietly as the truck lurched over potholes. The ride felt endless. Every bump sent a fresh wave of fear through my small frame. My mother never let go of Jun, her hands steady, her prayers a soft murmur against his skin. Amazingly, Jun remained conscious- he kept talking! Commenting on the trees we passed and how bumpy the road was.

When we reached the hospital, Jun was rushed straight into the operating room.

My father, who had just arrived at his office when he got word of the accident, jumped on his motorcycle, and raced back. He arrived while Jun was still in surgery. My mother was allowed to stay inside with the doctors, so my father and I waited outside.

He paced back and forth, unable to sit still, his face drawn with worry. Every now and then he would ask if I was thirsty or hungry. I shook my head. I knew something was terribly wrong.

"Where's the pair of your slippers?", my father asked, suddenly noticing that I was barefoot on one side.

"It got stuck in the tall grass when I was running to the road." I replied quietly. He nodded, as if that explained everything. "We'll get you a new pair", he said with a soft sigh.

After what felt like forever, the surgeon appeared with my mother, who looked eerily calm.

Jun was out of danger.

Only then did we learn how severe the injury had been: the javelin badly punctured his small intestines and the tip of one lung. Just an inch higher and it could have been fatal.

"It's a miracle," my mother breathed, thanking God over and over again for sparing her son. My father collapsed into a chair, burying his face in his hands, overcome with relief. I stood there silently, still not fully understanding but grasping enough. I was in awe- of the surgeon's skill, of my mother's faith, and of the strength it took to hold it all together.

Suddenly, I felt tired. The weight of the day settled on my little body.

My mother stayed with Jun at the hospital while my father took me to a relative's home on his motorcycle to rest. Jun had to be in the hospital for several days, so my mother filed for leave of absence to take care of him. Once Jun was out of the hospital, my mother filed for a transfer to another school in the town closer to her relatives. She received the transfer, so it was another new school and new Teachers Quarters. It would be in this area where we would settle and where my parents would eventually buy a property.

Jun survived. But the memory of his tiny body on the ground, of his guts spilling out, remained etched in our minds. He bore a jagged scar across his belly, a permanent badge of honor. As he grew older, he wore it proudly, spinning colorful stories to entertain friends- sometimes about being gored by a wild boar, other times about falling from a tree onto a sharp branch.

"But the real story's the best one," he'd grin. "It actually happened- and it gets the most laughs. Especially from my own family."

Even now, I marvel that he lived. And I cannot help but think about how helpless my father must have felt, as he pushed his motorcycle to its limit to make it to the hospital. That day changed all of us. In ways I didn't fully understand then, I knew- life could turn in an instant.

Looking back, it really did feel like a miracle that Jun survived. And in our family, miracles weren't just things you read about in the Bible- they were real, and they happened to people who prayed hard and believed even harder. Religion, like tradition, was a big part of our lives growing up. We went to Mass every single Sunday, no excuses. First Fridays too. And if there was a Holy Day of Obligation, we were there- Advent, Lent, feast days, all of it.

Every December, we woke up while it was still dark for Simbang Gabi- nine straight days of early morning Mass before Christmas. Sometimes we walked to church half-asleep, bundled up against the cold, our breaths fogging the air, but we never missed a day. It was just part of life.

There was one Simbang Gabi that I still remember, though probably not for the most pious reason. We were kneeling for the consecration, the moment when the altar servers rang the bells- then one of the bells flew off its handle and shot across the altar like a rogue comet. The poor altar server looked absolutely horrified! My friends and I saw the whole thing, and the giggles started- quiet at first, then uncontrollable. We tried to stifle them, but it was no use. We got a proper scolding, of course, but to this day, the memory makes me smile. Even in sacred spaces, life found a way to be hilariously imperfect.

Mama's faith, though, was unwavering. She prayed novenas like clockwork, crossed herself before every trip, and always thanked God out loud for both big blessings and tiny wins. After the accident, she just held Jun close and cried into his hair, whispering one prayer after another. And honestly, I believed those prayers had something to do with him making it through.

Faith was like that for us- it wasn't just about going to church. It lived in the background of everything we did, woven into our days like the rhythm of the seasons.

Yet even after near-tragedy, life marched on in all its small joys and daily rituals. We were amused by the simplest things. We laughed about the holes in our shoes, compared whose looked most like a funny face, and stretched our one pair of slippers as long as possible. Our clothes were mostly hand-me-downs, but my mother, with her prized Singer sewing machine, always made sure we looked presentable. "Just because we're poor doesn't mean we should act poor," she often said. As a child, I thought it must be something from the Bible.

Her lessons weren't always gentle. I learned that the hard way when I betrayed a friend's confidence and found myself at the center of a social disaster. Crying, I ran home, expecting my mother to comfort me.

Instead, she looked at me evenly and said, "You made a mistake. What was told to you in confidence should have stayed in confidence."

No soft words. No excuses. Just the truth. Her words stung at the time, but as I grew, I realized the depth of her wisdom. She taught me the value of trust and integrity, lessons that would guide me through many difficult decisions in life.

She was my third-grade teacher, and in the classroom, she commanded respect without ever raising her voice. I still remember the way the room would fall silent the moment she looked up from her desk, her quiet strength more powerful than any shout.

When your mother is your teacher, you'd think you'd get preferential treatment, right? Wrong! She treated me just like any of her students but always expected more from me. I believed I excelled in class and deserved the top honor, yet by the end of the school year, I was placed in third. I still remember the day after school started again when a classmate leaned in and whispered that I had been held back- not by chance, but because my mother had hoped I'd be number one. That remark embarrassed and confused me at the time. However, as I grew older, I came to understand it not as favoritism but as a subtle, tough-love lesson to push me to strive for even greater heights.

"You are not emotionally ready to move to the next grade," she said.

"What do you mean?" I retorted angrily. "I'm a good student!"

She agreed that I was and said I would understand later. I didn't say anything else, but I was mad- how could a mother do that to her child? I sat on the edge of the playground that first week, tracing lines in the dirt with a stick while my former classmates raced around the monkey bars. For a long time, I thought it was unnecessary. It took years before I realized what she did was out of love; she knew me better than I knew myself.

Some of her former students would visit her at school, and a few would chat with me about her strictness and high expectations. They said they hadn't appreciated it back then, but now they understood that without her guidance, many wouldn't have graduated elementary school, let alone gone on to college. I mostly nodded in agreement, though at the time, I stayed indifferent.

A woman- now also a teacher- once told me, "Your mom made me memorize a whole poem because I was caught cheating. I hated it then. But now? That poem helped me remember who I wanted to be."

I often think about those conversations and even find myself echoing her words. When my kids are searching for something and can't find it, I catch myself saying, "Use your eyes, not your mouth," and then smile as they roll their eyes just like I did.

I see her lessons everywhere- and I lean on them. Strength is not just about standing tall; it is about knowing when to listen, when to stay silent, and when to speak with conviction.

We thought we were just chasing puddles and hurling laughter into the wind, daring the rain to catch us. But now I see it differently. That muddy playground was a crucible. It held the joy of being wild and the cost of being careless, the thrill of freedom and the sting of its consequences.

In those rain-drenched afternoons and bloodstained evenings, something was being shaped in us- resilience, perhaps, or the early understanding that love and danger often dance close. My mother stood at the center of that truth, steady as a mountain in a storm. Her discipline was sharp, her mercy sharper. She stitched our wounds, scolded our recklessness, and never let go of the belief that we could grow into better versions of ourselves.

Looking back, those moments taught me to see the world in layers-poverty and abundance, strength and softness, beauty and brutality. It was in that muddy yard that I began to understand that life is rarely just one thing. Learning to live in that tension helped me endure, helped me transform.

What we mistook for play was preparation. And years later, when the rain came in other forms- judgment, shame, injustice- I found myself reaching back for the same grit, the same grace. And always, always, her voice.

And trouble, as it turned out, followed us- especially when our world shifted from the muddy comfort of the provinces to the blinding lights and long shadows of the city.

Chapter 3: City Lights, Shadow Lessons

"Ang hindi marunong lumingon sa pinanggalingan ay hindi makararat-ing sa paroroonan." ("He who does not look back to where he came from will never reach his destination.")

- Filipino proverb

Our family did not travel for vacations outside of our province when I was growing up. We simply couldn't afford it. But my mother instilled in me and my siblings the love of learning. She bought all the books by Dr. Seuss and My Bible Friends. As we got older, she shelled out a pretty penny for the hardbound Encyclopedia Britannica. "You cannot put a price tag on knowledge," she said much later when we asked her about it.

Those books became my window to the world. I loved the weight of each volume in my hands, the way the pages whispered as I turned them, and the faint smell of ink and old paper that clung to their spines. My mother had one rule: no dog-earing the pages. "Books deserve respect," she would say, handing us old greeting cards or folded ribbons to use as bookmarks. It felt ceremonial- like we were being taught not just how to read, but how to revere the written word.

Sometimes I'd sit cross-legged on the floor for hours, flipping from one country to the next, my fingers tracing maps and my imagination running wild. Outside our window, the view was always the same- mountains, sky, and endless fields- but inside those books, I was sailing the Nile, hiking through the Alps, and navigating the bustling streets of New York.

My siblings and I often sat side by side, each lost in our own volume, pointing out strange animals or flags we'd never seen before. "How do you say that?" one of us would ask, stumbling over a new word. Our mother didn't always know, but she would smile and say, "That's why we read."

And then there was Reader's Digest, stacked neatly beside the ency- clopedia, always worn from use. It featured stories of people who had made it- people who had built something from nothing. I don't remember their names, but their journeys stayed with me. I saw myself in them- their struggles, their grit. One day, I thought I would be successful like them.

Those weren't just childhood dreams. They were anchors. In a life that often felt uncertain, those stories told me that success wasn't just for people with money or privilege. It was for people who dared to imagine something more- and who refused to stop trying until they found it.

We read what we could get our hands on, from textbooks to fairy tale collections to Reader's Digest issues we reread until the corners curled. But nothing felt quite as magical as the arrival of the Encyclopedia Britannica. It made our home feel smarter, more serious-like we were preparing for something important. For a time, Bugsy and I even used it to quiz each other, flipping to random pages and challenging one another with obscure facts. We felt like scholars, even if we didn't always understand everything we were reading.

Looking back now, Bugsy and I often laugh (a little bitterly) about those volumes. Mama gave them all away- every single one of them- along with nearly every other book we grew up with. We sometimes joke that if we'd kept them, we might've sold them off by the volume or built a tiny library of our childhood.

There was one book I think about often, though I no longer remember the title. It came from a Dr. Seuss subscription, but I don't believe it was by Dr. Seuss himself. It was about a cyclist riding through a stunning mountain landscape- he might've been caught in a storm or just exhausted. He found shelter in a hostel and waited for the weather to pass. I don't even remember the ending. But to this day, whenever I drive through mountain roads or find myself gazing at pine-covered ridges, I think of that story. That one quiet, almost-forgotten book has never quite left me.

We were never short on stories- our lives were full of them, even when the pages were lost or given away.

But life had plans that would take us beyond the pages- farther than I ever expected.

The only time we ever left our province was out of necessity. My mother, determined to secure a promotion in rank and not just a permanent teaching position, needed to pursue continuing education. She was tired of being a substitute teacher, moving from one tempo- rary assignment to the next. I was about to enter fifth grade when we packed up our few belongings and, with everyone in tow, traveled to the next province over. By then, there were six of us: my parents, myself, my brother Jun, my sister Bugsy, and our youngest sibling, Chris, who was three years old.

We took a jeepney to our destination, a journey that lasted hours. As it rattled forward, the scenery shifted- lush fields and quiet mountains gave way to narrow roads lined with tightly packed houses. It was stifling hot inside the jeepney as we were packed like sardines. The seats had no cushions, so we felt every bump on the road. The smell of fresh earth and rice paddies faded, replaced by the exhaust fumes and street food. Every so often, our jeepney was stopped at a military checkpoint. At each one, we had to disembark while soldiers inspected the vehicle and our belongings before allowing us to continue.

My heart pounded every time we had to step out of the jeepney. The soldiers' eyes were cold, their hands firm on their rifles. I clutched my mother's hand, willing myself not to breathe too loudly, as if making a sound might draw unwanted attention. Those checkpoints terrified me. The soldiers, with their imposing rifles and unreadable expressions, were a constant reminder that the country was still under Martial Law. Then there were the resistance soldiers, will they come out shooting at these government soldiers? What would happen to us if that indeed happened? I tried not to think about that but each time we were stopped at a checkpoint, that thought crept back in my mind.

Back home, we would often see government soldiers patrolling our roads and highways. They sometimes would wander into our neighborhood; eyes alert and always on the ready. They were friendly but the mere sight of their rifles and their uniforms made me nervous. My mom always reminded us to just go about our business, to act normal. She would tell us the same thing when the rebel forces were out- act normal. For a kid, those statements made me more nervous than calm for reasons I couldn't understand then.

But the journey itself held dangers I had not yet understood. As a child, I thought little of the soldiers in our province- until we had to face them up close.

Then-President Ferdinand Marcos declared Martial Law when I was barely two years old. Growing up under its shadow, I often overheard hushed conversations about the dictatorship's atrocities. Stories of rebel forces clashing with the military, of people ambushed and killed, of politicians and activists disappearing without a trace. Though I was too young to fully grasp the dictatorship's grip, the chill in my spine during those checkpoints told me more than the hushed adult conversations could. And every so often, the reality of it struck close to home.

As a child, the world outside my doorstep was an endless playground- rice fields where I chased fireflies, rivers to splash in, trees to climb. I ran barefoot over dirt roads without a second thought, my laughter carried by the wind. The dangers of martial law were whispers in the background, things adults spoke of in hushed tones, warnings that sometimes faded beneath the thrill of adventure.

But then, something would snap me back. The sudden sight of soldiers patrolling the road, their rifles slung across their chests, their eyes scanning every passerby. My mother's hand tightening around mine as we walked past, her grip firm, a silent command to keep my head down. The way conversations would shift when a stranger approached- voices dropping, faces hardening, secrets swallowed mid-sentence.

Sometimes, it was a story whispered among my friends about a family that vanished overnight. Or a friend's neighbor whose house suddenly stood empty, open doors swinging in the breeze. Whether it was children's gossip or not, I didn't always understand the reasons, but I felt the weight of them, heavy like the humid air before a storm.

And yet, childhood had a stubborn way of reclaiming joy. One moment, I would be crouched behind a bush, playing patintero, giggling as I dodged my cousin's outstretched hand. The next, the sharp crack of gunfire in the distance would freeze us all in place, our breath held as we waited for the world to decide whether we could keep playing or force us to run and hide.

Even when I forgot, the world found ways to remind me.

One day, I learned that the older sister of my school friend had been killed. She had been riding home with her boyfriend, a soldier, when rebels ambushed their military convoy. The vehicle was set on fire, and she perished along with her boyfriend and his platoon. I attended her wake, and her casket was open for viewing. Through the glass, I saw a burnt body, barely recognizable as human.

I was taken aback- I had never seen a burnt body before. I hurried away from the casket, confused. A strange, acrid smell hung in the air, something I couldn't name, something foreign and unforgettable. Around me, there was the sound of hushed crying, and the grief felt like it clung to the walls. I told myself I should be sad, and yet all my young mind could muster was a single, stubborn question: is it really her in there? Even now, I wonder how they identified her remains. It was the 1980s, in a remote Philippine town- no DNA testing, no advanced forensics. Just charred memories and the stories people told themselves to survive.

On our way home, I tugged at my mother's hand and whispered the question aloud. "I don't know. Just pray for the family," she said gently. And I did. I prayed for my friend, for her sister, and for her family. But to this day, that question lingers, unanswered.

I have lost touch with my school friend, and I no longer remember her older sister's name, but that glimpse of scorched humanity is still etched into my bones. As I have gotten older, it has become the face of the detained, the exiled and the disappeared, resurfacing whenever I see a coffin, no matter how polished or pristine. It marked the end of something- childlike certainty, perhaps. That moment when nothing was ever innocent again.

After several military checkpoints, it was almost dark when we finally approached the city. Tired, I suddenly realized how far we were from our familiar surroundings, from home- it gave me an unsettling feeling but at the same time it got me excited to see what laid in front of us.

When we finally arrived in the city, I was overwhelmed. The bustling city streets were a world away from the tranquil terraces of my childhood. The city assaulted the senses; the silence of the terraces was replaced by the city's relentless hum. The air is thicker with smog and sweat. My siblings and I found wonderment in the new things we were discovering: the roads were wider and busier, the stores more plentiful, and the houses packed closer together. There was even a park with a lake where people rented rowboats- something I had only seen on TV. The sheer number of people was dizzying; they moved fast, and they spoke different languages. Thankfully, we could all communicate in English, a skill emphasized in school. Over time, I learned to speak their language too. I spent hours practicing with new friends, stumbling over unfamiliar sounds and phrases until they felt as natural as my native tongue.

The Philippines has no single official language, but rather two: Filipino and English. Filipino, derived from Tagalog, is the lingua franca in much of the country. English, a legacy of American colonial rule, is used for business, government, education, and media. With 120 to 180 languages spoken across the archipelago, linguistic diversity is deeply tied to geography and history.

Besides the new language, there was a different vibe in the city. People spoke louder and were outspoken with their likes and dislikes, more dramatic and animated. You would hear what is going on in their lives whether you liked it or not. Sometimes it felt like I was watching a soap opera! I used to tell my mother what I overheard from the neighbors, and she would caution me not to take part. "Gossip is a sinking ship. You don't want to be in it." She would say. As a child, it didn't really sink in, but it stuck with me. Often when I was growing up and I would find myself in a similar situation, I would repeat that line in my head. And, boy, it sure has saved me from many sticky situations!

The food was also different. The lowlanders, as we referred to those who are not from the mountains, did a lot more grilling. The scent of roasting peanuts mingled with the diesel fumes, the constant buzz of conversation a background hum as we navigated the bustling streets. I grew up with soup-based dishes, perhaps because it was colder in the mountains, so soup was necessary. They used more spices like black pepper and chili. My mother couldn't eat food with black pepper in it, never mind chili! She said she was allergic to it. I loved it! I started adding them to my food and overtime, I cooked with chili as well. What's not to like? That little kick has put some oomph in my cooking many years later!

For me and my siblings, moving to the city meant starting over. A new school, unfamiliar streets, and the challenge of making new friends all over again. My youngest brother Chris stayed home most days with a babysitter. My sister Bugsy, just in first grade, was still in her wide-eyed, carefree phase, unaware of the adjustments we all had to make. My brother Jun, ever the introspective and thoughtful one, took a bit more time to warm up to new people- but eventually, he did. As for me, I adapted quickly. I had always been curious and eager to learn, and I figured the best way to succeed in a new environment was to surround myself with classmates who were sharp and driven.

I gravitated toward a couple of bright girls in my class. At first, I quietly asked if I could sit with them during recess or join them in the library. They were kind, and they let me. Weeks passed, and one day, they invited me to the park. "Let's rent a rowboat and paddle around the lake," they said. My heart skipped- I had never done anything like that before! I rushed home and asked my mother if I could go. She saw the excitement in my eyes and didn't hesitate. "Yes," she said, and I beamed. That weekend, I climbed into a rowboat for the first time, surrounded by new friends, paddling through still water under the city sun. It was more than just fun- it was freedom. And in those quiet moments on the lake, I began to feel like I truly belonged.

These girls came from families that had much more than mine- nicer shoes, fancier snacks, and newer school supplies. One day, I admired a bracelet one of them was wearing. It sparkled when the light hit it, and I couldn't stop looking at it. She noticed and smiled, "You can borrow it for a couple of days if you want." I lit up. I was so flattered and excited that I said yes without thinking twice. I wore it proudly, holding up my wrist and watching it catch the sun as I walked. That bracelet made me feel pretty in a way I hadn't before.

When I got home, I showed it to my mom. "Look at this, Mom. Isn't it beautiful?" I said, holding my wrist up to her like I'd just come home from a ball. She studied it and nodded. "It is very pretty," she agreed. Then, her face softened. She set down whatever she was working on, turned to me fully, and said in her calm, thoughtful way, "If you don't own something, anak (child in English), that means you cannot afford it. And if you cannot afford it, holding onto it- even in your heart- will only disappoint you. One day, when you can afford beautiful things, you can choose what to buy. But for now, you must understand what is yours and what is not." I stared at her, puzzled. I didn't understand why she was trying to take this small moment of joy away.

Then she added, "Return the bracelet tomorrow. And when you do, make sure it is in even better condition than when you received it. That's how you show your gratitude and your character." I was disappointed, but I did what she said. I cleaned it carefully, checking for scratches, and returned it the next day with a smile. My friend was happy to have it back, and I felt a strange mix of pride and loss. I didn't fully understand what my mother was teaching me- not yet.

Years later, it all clicked. What she gave me that day was not just a lesson in manners- it was a blueprint for how to live with dignity and self-respect. Without lecturing, she had taught me that material things are never worth compromising your integrity. That craving what others have can quietly unravel your own peace. That the true measure of abundance is not what's on your wrist, but what's in your heart and how you carry yourself. The desire for more, when unchecked, can lead to unnecessary suffering: envy, debt, emptiness, and the hollow pursuit of appearances. Her lesson echoed louder the older I got.

My mother enrolled in college during that time, even as she raised four children and ran a household. My parents shared the daily tasks of feeding us, cleaning us up and putting us to bed. After that she would study deep into the night. My father, after stepping away from his steady teaching job, trained to become an insurance agent- a job that required him to travel long distances and face many uncertainties.

I didn't fully understand then just how much my parents were giving up for us- not just in money, but in spirit, comfort, and time. Only years later did small, quiet memories resurface with sharper meaning. Most nights, I watched my mother type into the early hours, my baby brother asleep in one arm, while my father sat beside her, silently helping cut and sort her handwritten notes. There were no speeches, no declarations of sacrifice- just two exhausted parents working by the glow of a single bulb, holding the line for a future we hadn't yet imagined.

With all the challenges my parents faced, somehow, they managed to send all three of us to a Catholic school, with our tuition subsidized by what must have been tireless efforts and sacrifices on their part. To this day, I still wonder how they pulled it off.

We were THE new kids, and we stood out in our poverty. Thankfully, school uniforms made it less obvious. Each of us owned two sets and a single pair of black shoes, which we wore until they practically disintegrated. Civilian clothes were reserved for weekends.

Despite the challenges, I liked the school. The student body was a mix of rich and poor, though the wealthy kids were easy to spot- they arrived in nice cars. The teachers were strict but fair. I liked all of them, but one in particular became my favorite. She was my English teacher, and it was under her guidance that my love for fiction truly blossomed. Mystery books, especially the Nancy Drew series, became my escape. I devoured the entire series in one year, captivated by the thrilling adventures and clever plots.

My sister Bugsy loves to remind me how Nancy Drew got me into trouble at home, a lot. I would get so engrossed in reading that I would forget to do my chores. "Remember when mom yelled your name, and you know how she doesn't like to repeat herself?" she would tease. We laugh about it now, but I'm sure it wasn't funny back then. My mother's strictness, especially when it came to chores, felt like the world's weight on my shoulders at the time, but looking back, I realize it helped shape my sense of responsibility.

My English teacher, Miss Paz, was no-nonsense and demanded excellence. She was the first to push me beyond what I thought I could do, especially when it came to writing. She had a particular way of encouraging us, always assigning essays that challenged us to think deeply. The best part was when she would pick her favorite essays and ask the students to read them aloud in class. I was picked several times, and each time, I felt a surge of pride.

One of the essays she asked us to write was "What are your favorite things to do?" I wrote about reading the Encyclopedia Britannica, how I would trace maps with my fingers and let the names of faraway places roll like poetry across my tongue. I imagined stepping into cities I couldn't pronounce and shaking hands with people I'd only seen in grainy black-and-white portraits. When I stood in front of the class to read my words aloud, my voice trembled- but the beating of my heart felt like a door opening. For the first time, I wasn't just a student. I was a storyteller. And someone was listening.

"That is beautiful," Miss Paz said, her eyes not leaving mine. "And if you do what needs to be done, you will see those beautiful places and meet those beautiful people."

Her words landed with the weight of a promise. In that quiet classroom, where the windows hummed with heat and chalk dust danced in the air, she gave me a gift I didn't know I needed- permission to dream, and the language to shape those dreams. It wasn't just about writing essays. It was about reaching beyond the horizon with nothing but a pencil and a voice that was finally learning to speak.

I never saw Miss Paz again after I left that school and went back home to the province. But sometimes, when I find myself standing at the edge of a new city, notebook in hand, I wish I could go back and tell her: I made it. I'm still writing. And I'm still chasing the beautiful.

One of the unique subjects offered was reading and comprehension. Each morning, we read a school paper- a small publication of current events- under a timer. Afterward, we took a quiz on the article. It was challenging but taught me to read quickly and understand context, an invaluable skill.

My math teacher thought I was good enough to enter the Regional Mathematics Tournament.

"You'll be great in the competition," my teacher encouraged, her eyes twinkling with pride.

I liked math, but I never thought I was really good at it. But, at that age I never shied away from challenges, so I agreed to enter. My parents, elated, brought me to the tournament. I never expected to make it to the finals, but I did! It was down to me and two other 6th graders. That was when I started feeling nervous. It has become real! My palms started to sweat, and I felt uneasy. The quiz master read the final math problem, then put the timer on. I was elated, I knew the answer! The buzzer came on and all three of us put down our pencils and raised our hands. The audience clapped, the tournament was over, the nail biting was over. The paper with our answers were picked up and checked.

I missed the answer because of a decimal point! I was in a hurry that I put the decimal point in the wrong spot! I was devastated! "What a stupid mistake!" I thought to myself, "Never again." I should have won the tournament or at least tied for first place. On the ride home, my parents were consoling me and at the same time congratulating me, "We're so proud of you! You were great! You made it to the finals!" Yeah, I thought, but I didn't win. That was the first time I felt the feeling of defeat, and I didn't like it! It felt like somebody gave me a piece of pie then snatched it back as I was biting into it. It was an unpleasant feeling, and it dawned on me how much I disliked losing. Perhaps that was the impetus of things to come, I like to win. This experience proved to me that I possess considerable aptitude and that I have the potential to excel in a field when I apply myself diligently. But that misplaced decimal point stayed with me for a while. Over the years as a student, each time I was in a rush to turn in my test papers, I would go through them one more time before I submitted them, making sure there were no "misplaced decimal points" to haunt me again.

Life, despite its hardships, had moments of sweetness. I had my first school crush there, a boy who made my heart flutter in ways I didn't quite understand yet. His name was Michael, and he was one of the rich kids in class. His parents dropped him off every morning in their shiny black car. Even as a young child, I understood that we were from two different worlds, so I tried hard not to let on, but my new friends noticed.

"You're staring at him again!" they'd tease.

"No, I am not!" I'd shoot back, flustered but secretly thrilled.

One afternoon, he approached me and my new friends whom he had known since first grade. "Is it okay if I walked home with you?" He asked, politely with almost a shy smile.

"Sure!" we said, trying to act casual.

I was giddy with excitement! I loved that almost-shy smile! Is this what growing up is? I wondered. Up until that point, I haven't fancied anyone. In school, I would steal a glance at him then looked away when he noticed that I was looking. The whole thing felt like a cat-and-mouse game, one that made me smile for no reason at all.

Nothing came of it, as school crushes often go, but I didn't know then how powerful that feeling could become- how it could grow, deepen, and one day, redirect my life in ways I couldn't yet imagine.

The city's energy swept me up before I had time to feel like an outsider. The clatter of jeepneys, the scent of street food curling through the air, and the constant hum of life felt less like something to figure out and more like something to join. I found my place in small ways- learning to haggle like I had always known how, laughing with new friends who never made me feel unexperienced, and moving through the streets as if they had always been mine to wander.

One Sunday after church, my father brought the whole family to a ten-pin bowling alley. We looked around, wide-eyed and confused by what we were walking into- but excited, with all the colored lights dancing above, filling the space. My siblings and I were in awe; we had never been in one before.

"Let's go rent bowling shoes," my father said, nodding toward the attendant.

"Why?" I asked.

"You'll see," he said with a grin.

Up to that moment, I had no idea what a bowling alley even was- never mind that my father knew how to bowl and was happy to teach us. I didn't realize then just how much I didn't yet know about him. But in that moment, we simply laughed at how badly we played, each time the ball found the gutter. The score didn't matter. We were together. And we were happy.

It was one of those small, luminous moments that made the city feel like a place of new beginnings- vibrant with the colorful fiestas for all occasions, Christmas, Easter, beauty pageants and singing contests, where even unfamiliar spaces held the potential for laughter, and where, for the first time, I saw my father not just as a parent, but as someone full of quiet surprises.

So, when I heard there was a singing contest in the plaza nearby, something in me stirred- that same sense of possibility, of stepping into something unknown but thrilling. I had never sung in a contest before, but a new song on the radio had captured my heart, and I wanted to sing it. I told my father, and to my delight, he was just as excited. We walked down to the plaza and entered my name.

There was only a couple of days to practice before the contest, so I made sure I memorized the lyrics and nailed the tune. The day arrived and my family and I went to the plaza. I was brimming with excitement! My parents were excited for me. My name got called, I walked to the stage and sang. I could hear the applause from the audience, and that made me feel good.

I didn't win, but I wasn't sad about it. My father was sad for me. He said I can try again next time. I never did try again. It's not because I didn't want to, or I was afraid to lose again. The interest just never piqued me again. I would still sing for fun, of course, over campfires and with school choir.

It is a head scratcher, that experience. I look back and I wonder why I was not nervous at all, before or during the competition. I once asked my mother if I was but forgot about it, and she said that I was confident, not nervous at all. Was that a prelude of things to come? Perhaps my confidence will one day land me in hot water, or hot waters? I don't know.

The city brought about new awareness and offered experiences I never could have imagined in my small town. It opened my eyes to contrasts-between wealth and want, privilege and struggle, silence, and speech. I saw how people navigated power, how some clung to it while others bore its weight. These encounters stirred something in me, a restless curiosity, a quiet fire. The city made me hungry- to see more, learn more, understand more. I was only 11 years old, and yet, the more I absorbed, the more I cherished the values and simplicity of where I came from. That small town of waterfalls and wild orchids had shaped me, anchored me. In the shadows and brightness of city life, I was beginning to see not just the world more clearly- but myself within it.

I also learned that the city's bright lights could cast long, dark shadows. We were told the war was far away, in the hills or on the news, but it found its way into our streets, our schoolyards, our wakes. It wasn't just something on the radio or whispered by grown-ups- it had a smell, a silence, a weight. And while I couldn't name it then, I had begun collecting shadow lessons- those quiet, complicated truths you carry without understanding until much later.

In time, I would come to know that my mother had been gathering her own shadows long before I was born, shielding us from their sharpest edges. But even she couldn't protect us from all of it- not the grief, not the questions, not the war.

Looking back now, I see how that moment- staring at the charred body behind the glass- marked more than just a memory. It was my first encounter with the human cost of the systems we lived under. I didn't yet have the language of politics or power, but I knew something wasn't right. That girl, someone's sister, someone's daughter, became a symbol of what could happen when violence was normalized, and war crept into our everyday lives.

Later, when I learned more about the Marcos regime, about Martial Law, and about how the state used fear to control, I began to place that memory in a broader frame. Her death wasn't random. It was part of the chaos sown by a dictatorship that fed off division and silence.

And still, that stubborn question remains: Is it really her in there?

Perhaps it does not matter. What matters is what that moment awakened in me- a desire to look closer, to question the stories we are told, to honor the forgotten. It's the same instinct that moved me several years later to sketch a sunrise behind broken chains. It's what helped me reclaim a sense of identity, a quiet confidence born not of innocence, but of awareness.

I didn't know then that these tensions- between safety and curiosity, between silence and truth- would one day shape how I saw the world, and how I moved through it.

One lesson in particular would come from someone I thought I knew best. My father's silence held its own stories- ones I hadn't learned how to ask.

Chapter 4: The House We Never Knew Existed and the Stream That Remembered

"It's not a house...It's a memory."
  -Toni Morrison, Beloved

Just as I was getting accustomed to our new life, my father surprised us with a visit to his childhood home- one we never even knew existed.

One day, my father announced we were visiting the place where he grew up- just outside the city. This confused us. Hadn't he grown up in the same province as my mother?

What we soon discovered was that my father had an entire past he had never spoken of- a world we were just being invited to glimpse. I thought I knew everything about him. But that visit would show me how much he had carried in silence.

When we arrived, we found ourselves in front of a sprawling property with a grand house. It was the biggest house I have ever seen at that point in my life! It had a wrap-around porch and was surrounded by large trees. As we walked into the vestibule, I was in awe! The room was bigger than our little apartment, and the ceiling rose above us like a cathedral.

My father called it a hacienda.

Inside, we were greeted by a woman respectfully referred to as "Mama." She wasn't his mother, and she looked different than us- her skin was lighter, her nose aquiline, and her frame fuller, perhaps softened by age. She carried herself with grace and elegance, her hair pinned neatly into a bun, not a strand out of place. A faint floral scent, like sampaguita or lavender, hung in the air when she moved. She held a pamaypay- an embroidered fan- close to her chest, the fabric fluttering slightly as it caught the breeze. She wore a subdued smile, and the way she looked at my father- proud, almost maternal- confused me. It reminded me of how my Lola, my dad's own mother, looked at him. My father was respectful, reverent even.

My mother stood quietly beside him, her expression unreadable, offering no further explanation. That silence puzzled me. There was a story here, but I didn't have the words or nerve to ask for it. Still, curiosity tugged at me.

She gave us a tour of the house. From the vestibule, we walked into the living room filled with plush sofas adorned with beautiful pillows. Traditionally, Spanish-influenced houses in the Philippines had expansive vestibules that doubled as ballrooms. These grand open spaces, often adorned with capiz shell windows, intricate woodwork, and soaring ceilings, were designed to impress. The furniture- elegant but practical- was arranged along the perimeter and easily pushed aside to make way for lavish gatherings.

The elite would arrive dressed in their finest barong – a traditional Filipino men's embroidered shirt, often worn for formal occasions, or terno – referring to the traditional Filipino women's matching top and skirt or now referring to the unique sleeve. Their laughter would echo off the polished Narra (the national tree of the Philippines) floors. Musicians played rondalla or flamenco, and the scent of lechon, pancit, paella and imported Spanish wine mingled in the air. These parties lasted until the wee hours of the morning.

Men like my father- house workers, caretakers, farmers- served every guest with quiet diligence. They poured drinks, cleared dishes, and fetched things without being asked. And when the last guest finally left, they collapsed into brief, broken sleep. By daybreak, they were already up again- scrubbing floors, preparing meals, toiling in the sugarcane fields. They rarely complained. They knew their place in the order of things.

It reminds me of stories about Southern plantations in the U.S- lavish, refined, and built on the labor of the unseen.

I didn't have the words for it then, but I felt it. The quiet heaviness in my father's eyes. The practiced stillness of my mother's expression. I was too young to name it, but even then, I sensed the weight of history pressing into the room like humidity- thick, clinging, and hard to shake. This wasn't just someone else's house. It was a symbol of something larger. And I was standing at the edge of it, trying to make sense of where we belonged. Even now, I can still recall the subtle discomfort in my chest, the way my instinct told me something was off- even before I had the language for it.

Later, when I learned more about our country's colonial past- how land was taken, how names were changed, how the illusion of class was maintained through servitude masked as loyalty- I looked back at that day with new eyes. My father's reverence, my mother's silence, even Mama's serene pride- they were all part of a story I was only just beginning to unravel. It made me wonder what else I had seen in my childhood that I didn't yet understand. The hacienda wasn't just a place. It was a memory etched with quiet power plays, silent sacrifices, and unspoken truths.

We walked into the living room filled with plush sofas adorned with beautiful pillows. They looked so comfortable! Then we entered the dining room. I could smell the scent of something fresh cooking in the kitchen behind it. The dining room table could sit over a dozen people! I have never seen a table that large and imposing. I wondered how many, if any, times my father sat at that table.

Until that moment, we had known nothing of this chapter of his life. My father, ever private, rarely volunteered information unless asked directly. We had assumed he had always lived in the same mountain province as my mother.

The woman, gracious and warm, welcomed us with open arms. She spoke fondly of my father, recounting how he had lived and worked there as a young man. Among the many helpers, he had stood out for his quiet diligence, earning her family's affection.

On the property, we explored an orchard. It was like we were back home in the forest, but not quite- there were no wild bushes or weeds growing around the trees, just neatly trimmed grass and the faint scent of ripening fruit in the air. The trees stood in perfect rows, their branches heavy with mangoes, guavas, avocados and coconut. Then there was the farm and- to my amazement- horses. We heard them before we saw them- snorting softly, hooves rhythmically striking the ground. I had never seen a horse in person before, only in books and on TV. Their sleek coats shimmered in the sun, their muscles rippling beneath as they moved. My father, sensing my fascination, offered to let us ride one. But we were too intimidated. I watched the horses from a distance, marveling at their power and grace, the way they held their heads high, tails flicking in the breeze.

Then we reached a nearby stream where my father said he used to swim. The air turned cooler under the shade of tall trees. I could hear the soft gurgle of water as it ran over smooth stones. I pictured him there as a younger man- splashing water, laughing, escaping the weight of work and responsibility, if only for a moment. He deserved that joy.

As we were leaving, "Mama" invited us to visit anytime, and my parents assured her that we would. She even gave us a couple of bags filled with the fruits from the orchard. With excitement, I reached for a ripe mango and started devouring it, the juices dripping on my fingers and my face was covered with it. It was delicious! My siblings looked at me with their eyes and mouth wide with shock and disbelief, and then they did the same thing. Normally, my mother would have said, "Wait until we get home." Or "Chew slowly, eat with manners." But this time, she let us be. She looked at us with a smile. I didn't know what she was thinking but I was glad not to be reprimanded.

Something about that day lingered with me. The way my father interacted with "Mama" was different- softer, more deferential. I didn't understand it fully then, but it planted questions in my mind. Who was she to him, really? And why had he never spoken of her before? Neither had my mother. And here in this large, beautiful house, my mother seemed so cool about it, not at all uncomfortable. She was friendly and respectful at the same time. Our mother had a self-assured and confident demeanor. It helped put us at ease in an otherwise awkward situation. My siblings and I never asked any questions- to this day I do not know why. Maybe we were too young. Maybe we didn't want to disturb something sacred. Or maybe, deep down, we knew certain answers came only when you were ready to carry them.

Looking back, that visit to the house we never knew was my first real encounter with opulence- grander than anything I'd imagined-, and oddly, with disparity. Until then, I knew we had little, but I never dwelled on it. We were fed, we were loved, we laughed. That was enough. But standing inside that grand house, with its high ceilings, polished floors, and elegant furnishings, it made the contrast more visible- more real. Something shifted in me. It wasn't just awe I felt- it was awareness. I noticed the disparity, yes- the carved wood, the plush furniture, the way the house seemed to float above the world. But I didn't feel small inside it. My mother used to say, "Don't waste your life comparing yourself to others. There will always be someone better off, and someone worse off. Focus on who you are becoming." That voice steadied me. We may not have had much, but we were loved, we were held, and that kind of wealth is harder to measure. With my awakening to the invisible lines that divided us, I began to wonder: Why do some people have so much while others scrape by with so little? Why is dignity so often tied to land, to ownership, to appearances? What made one family's name carry power while another's went unnoticed? I didn't have the language for it then, but the questions stayed with me, quietly reshaping how I saw the world.

I looked at him then- not as a father, not even as a man- but as a boy who once dove into that water, maybe to forget the weight of service, maybe to remember something of himself. It struck me that no matter how polished the world above might appear, here, in the quiet of the stream, he was just a boy again. And maybe, in that moment, I was too- trying to understand not just where we came from, but who we might still become.

Years later, I would return to that memory- not just of the house, but of the stream. It stays etched in my mind, not for its beauty, but for what it revealed: a kind of truth that lives beneath the surface of things. I didn't feel uncomfortable navigating the divide between wealth and want; my mother had always reminded us not to compare ourselves with others. She used to say, "Walk with humility, and never forget your worth." And in that quiet stream behind the grand house, I began to understand that class isn't only about money or titles- it's about proximity to power, about who gets to rest and who must keep swimming. But I also learned that grace could flow in any direction. My father had found his in the water. And standing there, I had begun to find mine.

We visited "mama" a few more times. I could see why my father treated her with reverence. The way she spoke with authority, she must have taught my father duty and perseverance. But her health was failing so her presence became scarce. Her personal maid told us that she wasn't feeling well, but to feel at home, nonetheless. But without her warm presence, the large house felt cold, uninviting. The few times we saw her; she looked pale and frail, and there was tangible sadness about her.

A few years after we went back to our province, my father received word that she passed away. He was devastated- and then surprised. He was asked to attend the reading of her will. The church was packed with her relatives and her workers. It was a solemn event, straight forward. After the service, my father, the relatives, and a few workers were called back to the house. The large vestibule was turned into almost a classroom with a large table in front of chairs arranged for the attendees. My father sat on a chair near the back of the room, still wondering why he was even there. Then he heard his name.

My father came home with heavy emotion but also ecstatic. He told my mother of his inheritance. "We finally have something of our own, free and clear!" he said, almost breathless with excitement. For a man who had worked his entire life for others, who had lived within the walls of houses that weren't his, this moment- this recognition- felt monumental. It wasn't just land; it was proof that his labor, loyalty, and silence had not gone unnoticed. It was dignity, written in deed and soil.

But that joy was short-lived.

When he returned to claim it, he learned that one of the ranch hands had sold the parcel out from under him. No one stopped it. No one informed him. The title slipped through his fingers as if it was never meant to be his at all.

He came home deflated. "My only inheritance is stolen," he told my mother, his voice tight, eyes clouded with disbelief and hurt. It was not just land that was lost, but the affirmation of a life's worth of sacrifices. The man who rarely spoke of injustice now moved with less purpose, shoulders heavier, silences longer. He still woke early, still worked hard, but something had shifted. His pride- once unshakeable- felt bruised, like a banner slightly torn but still flying.

My mother, always the wiser of the two, told him softly, "It wasn't meant to be." Her words were kind, but I saw the ache behind them. She knew how much that land meant to him- not for wealth, but for what it symbolized: roots, permanence, legacy.

I didn't fully grasp it then, but I know now that inheritance is not always material. Sometimes it's a wound that is passed down quietly, a story unfinished, or a dream deferred. My father's inheritance became mine in that way. I inherited the ache of that lost land, the knowledge that even when you earn something ten times over, it can still be taken from you if you were never meant to have it. And yet, I also inherited his quiet strength- the resolve to continue, to rebuild without bitterness, to continue believing in the worth of one's labor, even when the world refuses to acknowledge it.

That loss stayed with him. But so did his dignity!

Perhaps it was that lingering sense of loss, tempered by quiet dignity, which led him- years after retirement- to join a grassroots movement in our province and beyond, fighting for the rights to agricultural land. He marched in protests, raised his voice at the capitol steps, and along with other members of the movement, was even jailed for a week. My mother bailed him out, without much fuss. From that collective effort, several families were able to reclaim land once seized by the government under eminent domain. My father received a small parcel of land-just enough to plant corn and other crops. It became his refuge, a place where he could work the soil once again, as he had done as a young boy. Only this time, the land was his. Hard-won, yes- but wholly his. Earned not only through labor, but through conviction, solidarity, and the stubborn kind of hope that refuses to die.

After my mother completed her studies, we returned to our province.

By then, I had graduated from elementary school and was preparing for high school. My siblings returned to our old elementary school.

Watching my mother take on the challenge of going back to school to pursue what she wanted while taking care of her young family made me realize that nothing is given to you. You have to go after what you want- with everything you have. In pursuit of that, you need a partner who will support you no matter what. I don't think she would have done it without my father's quiet, unwavering belief in her. My father, who turned out to be a man of resolve and strength deeper than he ever showed. As I got older, whenever the stress of daily life weighed on him, I would think back to that young boy who left behind everything and everyone he knew in pursuit of a better life. And in those moments, I was reminded of his strength, etched in silence, not spectacle.

Life had come full circle, but the experiences of those two years stayed with me. They have given me perspective- on life beyond my province, on the nuances of privilege and survival, on what it means to find your footing in unfamiliar terrain. That visit to the house we never knew opened a quiet awareness in me. It was my first brush with opulence, and with it, the first real understanding of disparity. Until then, I never questioned our lack- we had love, we had laughter. But seeing luxury up close made the contrast unmistakable. And yet, I never felt out of place. My mother always said, "Never compare yourself to others. There will always be someone better, and someone worse. Just be better than you were yesterday." It was a lesson that became a compass.

And so, I carried that lesson with me to the stream behind the house, where the world slowed down. I remember crouching by the water's edge, the coolness of the stones beneath my hands, the murmur of the current slipping over rock and root. My father had once swum there as a boy, and as I stood in the shade of the same trees, I tried to imagine him- lighter, freer, if only for a moment. That stream, nestled in silence, held a kind of memory I could almost touch. A boy who toiled for others. A man who would one day fight for what was his. And a girl, me, learning that strength isn't just in what you survive, but in how you keep dreaming anyway.

That water, cool and quiet, didn't just reflect the sky- it reflected truth: we were all trying to return to something unburdened, something free.

Chapter 5: Sharp Knives and The Language of Eyes

"Who needs thunder when a look can split the sky."
-Unknown

My mother, the second of twelve siblings, grew up in a small town a few hours from where I grew up, surrounded by terraced rice fields that stretched high into the mountains. The creeks and springs that irrigated the fields produced a constant, rippling murmur- like a gentle, musical burble that blended with the sounds of rural life. I still recall the cool mist that would settle over the terraces at dawn- the air carrying a hint of jasmine mixed with the aroma of wet soil. It was the sensory symphony that marked the start of each day.

The three main occupations in the province at that time were farming, weaving and wood carving. Her parents- my grandparents- were farmers, like most in their community. The fields were accessible only by traversing narrow paths and crossing streams; the nearest road lay at the base of the mountain, hours away by foot. From there, you could catch a bus or jeepney to reach your destination. The isolation of her town shaped her childhood, grounding her in both the beauty and hardship of rural life.

Typical Ifugao Village, picture taken by my son Mark in 2022

Some of her siblings learned the art of wood carving, a trade that remains central to the area today. Traditionally in our province, Ifugao, wood carving is most notably known for the creation of the bulul figures, often depicting human figures representing ancestral spirits guarding the rice crops. They are also considered a symbol of wealth and prosperity. Wood carving as an industry has since evolved to include other figures. Some are animals; some are figurines, to something as intricate as a bust in the image of whoever commissioned the work.

Ifugao weaving, now a highly regarded and culturally significant art form in the Philippines, is practiced primarily by women. It involves intricate patterns and symbols, often incorporating traditional rituals and techniques like ikat dyeing. This technique involves tying and dyeing the yarn before weaving, resulting in distinctive, blurry patterns.

My mother, however, found wood carving to be too meticulous and weaving too back breaking so she dedicated herself to farming, which, ironically, is both. The family's livelihood depended on rice, with vegetables planted between seasons. From an early age, she worked alongside her parents and siblings, tilling the land, planting, and harvesting. I remember her recounting how, during a particularly harsh dry season, she and her siblings would wake before sunrise, determined to irrigate their field with every drop of water they could find. Her voice trembled while she described the back breaking nature of farm work, yet her eyes sparkled with pride for what she and her siblings accomplished.

Farming practice in my province is wet-rice cultivation and swidden agriculture. A native white glutinous rice called tinawon, also known as Ifugao heirloom rice, a long season rice variety planted December to February after the rainy season ends; then after the harvest, vegetables are planted in place of the rice stalks. Tinawon rice is prized for its nutritional value, unique aroma and texture, leading to high demand both nationally and internationally. Tinawon literally means once a year, and it was indeed planted- once a year, making it a distinct and valued crop in the Philippines. The farmers believed that it was the best way to sustainably farm the land. They practice seasonal cycles of planting, natural pest control and manual harvesting, no machineries or commercial fertilizers. Their challenges then and now are weather related. The warm months can bring drought, and the rainy season can be heavy and can cause landslides. Today, added to that is the lack of interest of the younger generation to continue the tradition. There is also the constant pressure from large corporations to increase the harvest to more than once a year by using artificial fertilizers and harmful pesticides. And yet, they stand strong in their proven farming practice and persevere, year in and year out.

My mother's life oscillated between farm work and school, a demanding routine that left little room for leisure. Getting to school was a challenge in itself. Transportation was rare, and money for fares even rarer. Rain or shine, my mother and her friends walked over an hour each way, often arriving at class drenched by torrential tropical rains that no umbrella could fend off. I can only imagine how uncomfortable it must have been to sit through lessons in soaked clothing. Yet, she persevered, and at 12 years old, her determination earned her a spot at a Catholic high school, thanks to her good grades.

In high school, she lived in the convent dormitory during the school week, returning home on weekends. Each Sunday afternoon, she and her friends walked for hours from their village to the town where their school was, carrying provisions of yam, rice, a few vegetables, and pieces of firewood. These supplies were given to the dormitory matron for the common mess, shared among all the occupants, including the nuns. Whenever necessary, the nuns would supplement their meals.

During the school week, in exchange for free board and lodging, she helped clean the convent and wash clothes and dishes. This was no small feat- without modern conveniences like dishwashers or washing machines, every task was done by hand. Each morning at 4 a.m., she and her friends woke up, collect freshly baked bread, and walk to town to sell it to the townspeople. The bread was made by the boys in the boys' dormitory, who were also self-supporting.

The freshly baked bread was placed in wicker baskets, covered with cloths, then they walked the streets calling out, "Pan-de-sal!" announcing to the neighborhood that the warm, fluffy rolls had arrived. They rarely returned to the convent with leftovers. The scent of warm yeast and toasted crust wafted through the streets before they even spoke, drawing sleepy townsfolk to their doors with coins in hand. On the rare days, they would share the remaining bread among themselves, savoring its warmth and comfort after a long morning's work.

The convent is a world of its own- quiet corridors filled with faint scent of incense and the steady hum of prayers. Each morning, as she rose at 4am, I imagine she steeled herself for the day ahead by first praying, then balancing the weight of academic expectations with the grueling tasks of daily labor.

Each Friday afternoon, she and her friends would make the 3-hour trek back to their village. Along the way, they would pick fresh fruits, mangoes, avocadoes, and bananas, happily eating some but always saving a few as a treat for their siblings. "Those are the memories I cherish the most," she once told me. That, and the care and guidance she received from the nuns, who also provided her with clothes and footwear- a true luxury at a time when almost everyone walked barefoot.

Higher education was an even greater challenge. In those days, a quality college education required attending private or parochial schools, most of which were Catholic institutions run by Belgian priests and Dutch nuns. The nearest college was hours away, in another province, and attending meant leaving her family for long stretches. Despite the distance and financial strain, her parents gave her their blessing, knowing it was her best chance for a brighter future. However, they couldn't afford to support her studies.

In many ways, my mother was a recipient of an early version of a Diversity, Equality and Inclusion (DEI) initiative. At that time, the Catholic Mission had a Study Now Pay Later program championed by Reverend Father Gerard de Boeck, a Belgian priest. He saw in my mother and two other bright, indigent native students the potential and gave them the nudge they needed. The three of them were the first ever Indigenous students accepted in that program. Without him, my mother might never have attended college.

Much like the Native Americans, the Indigenous people of the Philippine Mountain provinces were looked down upon. The Spaniards, unable to conquer them by force- thanks to their fierce resistance- resorted to vilifying them instead. When guns failed, they turned to religion. That is how my mother and her family became Christians- by conversion, not conquest, or perhaps somewhere in between.

The Dutch nuns were strict but also instilled invaluable lessons. They taught her proper etiquette- how to speak politely, dine with grace, and carry herself with dignity. "Don't speak with your mouth full," they would say. "Wait your turn to speak. Look people in the eye when addressing them." These lessons extended beyond manners, offering wisdom that helped her navigate life's challenges. She passed these principles on to me and my siblings, shaping our upbringing in profound ways.

These early lessons in discipline and dignity didn't just mold her- they became the foundation upon which our family was built. Her quiet strength and steadfast values would echo through our lives, even when

I was too young to understand.

When she was telling me and my siblings how she managed to secure the nun's confidence, she related it with a sense of accomplishment. She didn't downplay the difficulty, but she didn't complain about it either. "It was just the way it was." She would say. I always wondered how strong and determined she must have been as a child to have the courage to do what no one in her family at that time had ever done.

My mother graduated with a two-year teaching course and received an Elementary Teachers Certificate (ETC). She was only 18 years old when she started her first teaching job. She was excited at the prospect of starting something for herself, a new career. There was a gleam in her eyes when she spoke about her first classroom- the smell of chalk, the shuffle of tiny feet, the awe of being called "Ma'am." It wasn't just a job. It was the first time she saw herself not as someone's daughter or sister, but as her own person. At the same time, she was nervous; nervous because it was her first time teaching a group of children, nervous also because of the enormity of the responsibility of molding young minds to be thinkers and self-sufficient as good and productive members of society. But she was also confident in herself, confident that with God's help, she will do well in carrying out that responsibility.

Her faith, deeply rooted in Catholicism, was her anchor. She attended church regularly and believed in the power of prayer, trusting that God would provide. As she took my siblings and me to church, I would see her face light up as she listened to the words of God being spoken by the priests. I could see in her face that she truly is a believer, a woman of faith. She wasn't preachy but lived her faith quietly, embodying kindness and charity. Her generosity was boundless, often to a fault.

She never met a stranger and always extended help, even when it stretched our family's resources thin.

As the first in her family to earn a degree, my mother felt a deep responsibility to support her younger siblings and parents. Her eldest sibling had married young, leaving her to shoulder the role of family caretaker. Over the years, one or more of her siblings often lived with us. Our homes were modest- usually rented or provided by the school system- but my mother welcomed them with open arms. Space was tight, and resources were stretched, but she treated them like her own children. To this day, one of her siblings affectionately calls her "Mama".

Of course, she wasn't without flaws. She could be impatient. I remember when her younger siblings stayed out too late or didn't do what she asked them to do. She would be right at the door when they got home, with a steely gaze and with a low voice quizzing them. She also had a knack for repetition- if she told you something once, she'd tell you a hundred times. She rarely raised her voice, but she had a tone and a look that conveyed everything you needed to know you were in trouble. Sometimes, she didn't need to say anything at all; her silence was enough. Have you ever heard the phrase "if looks could kill"? With just a look, she could slice you open. We used to call it her "dagger eyes"- cold, sharp, and full of warning. Words weren't always necessary.

She lost her cool a few times with my siblings and me, and one incident stands out in my mind. One afternoon, my mother told us to take a nap while she and our father ran errands. We said yes and lay down as they were leaving. As soon as they left, we got up, looked at each other with a knowing smile- full of mischief -, then went out to the backyard and played instead. We were having so much fun and so engrossed with whatever we were doing that we didn't realize our parents were back.

"Get inside!" we heard our mother. We instantly ran into the house, worried. "You didn't do what I told you to do! Get in line!"

She lined us up from oldest to youngest, and spanked us, one after the other. It didn't even hurt, but the two little ones, Bugsy and Chris, were crying, and their shirts were soaked with tears and snot. They looked so helpless. I thought they were more scared than hurt and I felt really bad about it. I realized I shouldn't put my siblings in that situation again, and I didn't. Now, we talk about it and laugh. Getting spanked as a group sounds funny now, it wasn't funny then.

But there was one time that she totally lost her temper- and boy did she! I remember it vividly.

We were living in the Teachers Quarters, and it was around the same time when my brother Jun was hit by a javelin. One of my mother's younger sisters, my Aunt Maya, was living with us then. She was a vivacious and precocious young girl. You rarely ever saw her without a smile on her face, and I enjoyed her company! I was outside playing with my friends when suddenly, the front door flew wide open. Bang!

"How dare you embarrass me? Get out of here!" Startled, I turned around to see my aunt crying and my mother right behind her, scolding her and pushing her out the door. "It wasn't me! I didn't do it!", my aunt said, sobbing as she ran out to the school grounds.

We later found out that one of the teachers living in the Quarters had accused my aunt of stealing money from her room. My aunt, of course, denied it. I do not recall if it was ever resolved, but that incident remained etched in my memory. I have never seen my mother, before or since, lose her temper that way. It actually scared me a little bit. It was the first time that I realized that my mother can be fearsome. It was hard to square that moment with the calm, composed woman shaped by nuns and scripture. But maybe grace and fury weren't opposites after all- just two sides of the same strength. As a little girl, it also put me on notice, stealing is not a good thing.

As the oldest child, I bore responsibilities my younger siblings didn't. I cooked, cleaned, and helped with the laundry, often feeling the weight of these duties more acutely than them. I remember one incident vividly. I was outside playing when my mother called me to gather the dry clothes from the line. Grumbling under my breath, I stomped inside, muttering about the unfairness of it all- why was I always the one doing chores? Sitting across from me, my mother quietly sewed, pretending not to hear my complaints. Her silence spoke volumes. I don't recall what I did next, but the memory of her calm, unspoken disapproval has stayed with me.

My mother valued integrity and discouraged gossip. Her ability to navigate social situations with quiet finesse was remarkable. Without saying a word, she could diffuse tension with a single, knowing smile- a smile that softened the air, lowered defenses, and reset the room's temperature. She often reminded us of the adage, "Great minds discuss ideas; average minds discuss events; small minds discuss people." She lived by this principle, never indulging in idle talk. Instead, she chose kindness and understanding, modeling them in both words and deed.

One thing my mother couldn't stand was conflict, especially between my brother Jun and me. We fought constantly, arguing over the smallest things. She would warn us that if we didn't stop, she would leave us. Once, in a moment of exasperation, she handed us knives and said, "If you really hate each other, here. Kill each other!"

Jun and I froze, eyes locked, steak knives poised mid-air like we were in a low-budget Western. The fluorescent kitchen light buzzed above us, casting sharp shadows on the concrete floor. I could hear the ticking of the wall clock, each second louder than the last, like a countdown to something ridiculous. My hand gripped the knife's plastic handle so tight my fingers were going numb, but I didn't dare move. Jun looked at me with wide eyes, his face pale and lips twitching- not sure if he was about to burst out laughing or burst into tears. I knew my own face must have mirrored the same mix of horror and disbelief.

We didn't need to say anything. The message was clear: She's absolutely serious. She will actually make us kill each other if we kept this up. That realization hit like cold water to the face. Slowly, in perfect unison, we lowered our weapons, set them gently on the kitchen counter like they were explosives, and backed away. I think one of us muttered something like, "Do you want to find our friends and play outside?"

From that day forward, we still argued- of course we did- but the threat of maternal-sanctioned murder kept it firmly in the PG zone. We also never fought in front of her again, and she never brought it up. Something unspoken shifted between us. We still bickered, but less like enemies and more like conspirators- two kids who had seen the edge of something absurd and lived to laugh about it. Now my siblings and I would laugh about it. My sister Bugsy especially. She, more than anyone in the family, would remind us all. She would even mention it to our mother.

"Mom, remember when you gave Jane- my nickname then- and Jun a knife when they were fighting? You said "here, kill each other!", Bugsy would say, laughing. "Oh, that!", my mother would say as she joined everyone in laughter.

As vivid as those moments were, equally unforgettable were her "curing" techniques.

Whenever one of us was down with a cough or congestion, she'd grab a betel nut leaf, wilt it over fire, and gently press it to our chest.

"What's that for, Mom?"

"This helps loosen the phlegm so it's easier to expel," she'd say.

"Can't you just use Vicks?"

"Yes, but this is natural, it works just as well, and it's not messy."

For stomach aches, she brewed ginger tea instead of handing us Maalox. For headaches, she pressed on pressure points in our fingers. I once asked her how she knew all this. "Some of it I learned from tradition," she said. "Some from the Dutch nuns."

Looking back now, I think that was my first real introduction to natural wellness. I didn't fully realize it until years later, when I became a certified yoga instructor. Those "curing" moments seeped into my subconscious: how so much of what I saw her do had quietly become the foundation of how I live and heal today.

My mother's unique approach to teaching her children life lessons and to life itself was shaped by her upbringing in the convent and the wisdom of the Dutch nuns. She endured hardships with grace and imparted invaluable lessons to her children. Through her sacrifices, faith, and unwavering strength, she taught us the true meaning of resilience and love.

Knives and dagger eyes- sharpened over decades of motherhood and wielded with terrifying precision. She didn't need to yell. One glance could shut down a tantrum, a smart mouth, or even a teenage rebellion. Honestly, I'm still not sure if she had laser vision or just decades of Catholic guilt baked into her glare.

Looking back, I see how every hardship she endured, every sacrifice she made, was not only for survival but also to light a path for the rest of us. I would later find that, in moments of challenge- whether when a test seemed insurmountable or when faced with rejection- there was a quiet voice inside me echoing her steady, measured advice. In those moments, I realized that her determination had seeped into my very being, guiding me even when I couldn't see the way forward.

In her silence, her stare, her stories, she taught us how to endure- and how to rise above, with our own sharpened edges softened only by love. In her quiet fortitude, she taught us the emotional and mental continence to withstand and overcome. It wasn't through grand declarations or sweeping gestures, but in the way she moved through the world: steady, composed, quietly anchoring those around her. Her lessons weren't spoken aloud- they were embedded in how she held herself in hardship, how she offered grace instead of gossip, strength instead of spectacle.

We didn't just learn resilience- we absorbed it, watching her rebuild from silence, hold the line with grace, and choose dignity over despair. But outside the walls of our home, where values were shaped less by quiet strength and more by colonial legacies, another set of lessons waited for us- less kind, less just. Lessons about beauty, worth, and who gets to belong. It was there, beyond our mother's gaze, that I began to understand how some forms of power are inherited not through wisdom, but through skin color.

Chapter 6: The Whiter the Better

"All animals are equal, but some animals are more equal than others."
  -George Orwell, Animal Farm

While my mother learned life lessons and skills in a convent, my father learned his under the punishing heat of the sun.

Before the sun rose over the sugarcane fields, my father would already be awake. The scent of boiled rice, the low hum of morning chores, and the distant crowing of roosters marked the beginning of another day of work and study. He was still a boy then, but the weight he carried was already that of a man.

My father is the second child in a family of five. Like my mother, he grew up in similar circumstances- poor, from a small rural town, and only accessible by foot from the nearest road. His childhood was one of simplicity, with little more than the land and the tight-knit community he called home. He went to a public elementary school, where education was a privilege, and beyond that, opportunities were limited.

After finishing elementary school, his life took a sharp turn. He was sent to live with a wealthy family of landowners in a neighboring province- a world away from the simplicity of his rural home. There he could work and go to high school at the same time. It wasn't what he wanted; he felt the same trepidation any young person would in his place. But that was the only way he could continue his education. At that time, his older brother was heading to college and their parents- my grandparents- could hardly afford to send one to school, never mind two. So, he resigned himself to the idea.

There, on a sprawling hacienda stretching as far as the eye could see, his days began to fill with both hard labor and the promise of education. My father's role was to serve as a house and farm helper. In return for his labor- cooking, cleaning, washing clothes, and working the fields- the family promised to send him to school. To relax, he would swim in the nearby river. It wasn't much of a river- more like a shy stream winding its way through tall grasses and smooth stones. But to him, it was a sanctuary. The cool water against his sunburnt skin brought instant relief after long days of cooking, cleaning, and toiling in the fields. He loved swimming! It was his escape. Out there, with only the sound of rippling water and rustling leaves, he could just be- a boy suspended between the weight of work and the quiet freedom of the water.

And yet, he never taught us how to swim. Never even mentioned it. I still wonder why. Maybe the rivers of his youth felt too far away by the time we came along- flowing somewhere downhill from the life he had to climb. Or maybe, life was simply too busy. Still, as a child, I sometimes imagined what it might've been like- him lifting us into the water, showing us how to float, laughing as we splashed around. But those moments only lived in my daydreams. He had left that river far behind.

Maybe he never taught us to swim because he didn't want to remember the boy who once could. Or maybe that river belonged to a self he had no way to carry forward.

For several years, my father worked diligently on the hacienda, tending to the land and helping with household chores, all while receiving his education in a place far from his family.

To understand my father's world, you have to understand the system that shaped it- a legacy of Spanish colonization that outlasted the colonizers themselves. What is a hacienda, you might ask?

The first Spaniards set foot in the Philippines in March 1521, but it wasn't until 1565 that the official colonization began. The Spanish occupation lasted until 1898, when the United States emerged victorious in the Spanish-American War and Spain ceded the Philippines to the United States. During the Spanish occupation, the Spaniards introduced Christianity and the hacienda system to the islands.

The hacienda system was born out of Spanish colonial policies and later continued under American rule. The Spanish established large estates, or haciendas, which were used to cultivate crops and generate wealth for the colonizers. These estates were often worked by the local native population, many of whom were forced into labor under harsh conditions. Haciendas were not just agricultural units; they were centers of control, where the local community was bound to the land and its owners in a system that limited their freedom and economic mobility.

When the United States took control of the Philippines, they maintained and expanded the hacienda system. Under American rule, the

Philippines became a major supplier of raw materials, particularly sugar, to the United States. This led to the rise of corporate mono-crop plantations, where vast tracts of land were dedicated to a single crop, often sugar, in order to meet the high demand for export. These plantations were managed through the same exploitative system, ensuring that the local population continued to work the land under conditions that were little better than before.

These weren't just farms. They were hierarchies carved into the soil, where laborers bent under the weight of both harvest and history.

The mornings started before the first light of dawn. My father would wake to the sound of roosters crowing and the rustling of house helpers already busy with their morning chores. The wooden floors of the house creaked beneath his feet as he hurried to the kitchen, where the warmth of the clay stove and the scent of boiling rice filled the air. He would prepare food for the landowners first, carefully setting out their breakfast- hot chocolate thick with sugar, pan de sal still warm from the oven, eggs fried in lard. Only after they had eaten could the servants have their own meal, often nothing more than rice with tuyo, a small, sun-dried fish so salty it made the lips pucker.

The days were long and grueling. The sun bore down mercilessly, turning the fields into an endless sea of gold. The air shimmered with heat, and the dust clung to his skin as he worked. The sugarcane leaves were sharp, slicing into the arms of workers as they harvested the tall stalks. When the wind blew, it carried the scent of burning husks from the sugar mills, a thick, smoky sweetness that clung to everything.

The relentless sun scorched the fields, sweat mixing with the earthy scent of sugarcane. I imagine my father's heart must have pounded with a mix of determination and melancholy- knowing that every clump of dirt he turned was a step away from his own family's warmth, yet also a step toward a future he could only dream of.

The hacienda was a world of its own, where hierarchy was unspoken but deeply understood. He quickly learned his place. In the house, he moved silently, careful not to make unnecessary noise in the presence of the landowners. He kept his own counsel, spoke when necessary, answering only when required. Outside, among the workers, the rules were different but just as rigid. The farmhands, their backs permanently bent from years of toil, regarded house helpers with a mix of envy and quiet resentment. They all understood that to work indoors was to have a slightly better life- a roof over one's head, access to cleaner clothes, and most of all, a chance to be seen as something more than just another laborer.

At night, exhaustion settled deep in his bones. The wooden cot he slept on was rough, the woven banig mat doing little to cushion his aching muscles. The scent of smoke and sweat lingered on his clothes, and the calluses on his hands told the story of each day's labor. But in the dim light of the kerosene lamp, he studied. The pages of his schoolbooks smelled of old paper and dust, the ink smudged from hands that had been in the fields all day. He fought against sleep, pushing himself to read just one more page, write just one more answer.

For a young person in high school, this was his life- a cycle of work, study, and exhaustion. But there was always a quiet fire in him, a determination that would not be dulled by hardship. He knew education was his only way out. And so, he endured.

Those long, exhausting days on the hacienda not only honed his work ethic but also instilled in him a quiet resolve that would guide his later journey- a resolve that would eventually lead him from fields to the classroom, and from hardship to a modest promise of a different life.

He eventually left the hacienda to focus on college. Grueling manual labor left him too exhausted to focus on his studies. By that time, his older brother had finished college and had a job. So, he turned to his older brother, who agreed to support him financially. But it was still difficult to make ends meet so he took a job at a funeral parlor to augment the money his brother was giving him.

According to my mother, he disliked the job. Being around bereaved families wasn't enjoyable. It was a world away from the hacienda in more ways than one, but the struggle was still the same. Work, school, study- then do it all over again until he finally earned his degree in education.

In many ways, my father's experience on the hacienda was a reflection of this larger historical context, a microcosm of the struggles that many Filipinos faced during that era. It was a world where the privileges of the wealthy were built on the labor of the poor, and the hope for a better life was tied to the land they worked.

The hacienda system created complex class and caste dynamics between Spanish colonists, wealthy landowners, and laborers. These divisions persisted long after the Philippines gained nominal independence from the United States in 1946. The effects of these hierarchical structures, rooted in Spanish colonialism, had far-reaching consequences, creating a society where even within a single class, there were layers of distinction- often based on skin color, lineage, and occupation. These caste-like dynamics shaped everything from personal identity to social interactions, and they still lingered in subtle ways long after the formal end of colonial rule.

As I grew older, my father shared stories of life in the hacienda, offering a glimpse into the rigid social order that governed every aspect of daily life. I remember his story where he would sometimes lower his eyes when speaking with the landowners, a silent acknowledgment of his place in that rigid social order. Even as a child, I sensed that the weight of those expectations had molded him- a burden that would follow him yet also fuel his relentless pursuit of education and dignity.

He told me that within the labor class itself, there was a strict hierarchy. House helpers were considered of higher rank than farm workers. The division was so clear that farm workers would vie for the coveted position of house helper, seeing it as a way to gain status and a better life. The role of house helper was not just about the work itself- it was about being closer to the family, living inside the house rather than out in the fields, and- most importantly- being lighter in complexion.

The preference for lighter skin was a direct reflection of the belief that fairer skin was associated with higher status. It was a deeply ingrained part of Filipino culture, rooted in centuries of Spanish colonial rule, where lighter skin was associated with mestizos, those of mixed Spanish and Filipino heritage, who were often seen as more beautiful and refined than the full-blooded natives. This notion permeated every aspect of life, from marriage to beauty standards, and it gave rise to the saying, "the whiter the better," which reflected the belief that a lighter complexion signified a higher social rank. House helpers, typically lighter in skin because they worked indoors, were considered superior to the darker farm workers who toiled under the sun. My father, having been a farm worker before his time as a house helper, knew this well.

Though my father worked tirelessly to carve a better future for himself, the biases he faced didn't disappear - they simply evolved, persisting in ways I wouldn't fully grasp until later. I was too young to understand it at the time, but I would soon come to realize that the same prejudices that shaped his life would also leave their mark on mine.

One day in school, a friend remarked casually on how dark I was. I thought it was strange, but I let it pass. Only later did I realize it wasn't just a comment- it was a cue. A reminder of where I stood in a world still shaped by caste-like legacies of color and class. Even my father, who had earned a degree in education- who had clawed his way from hacienda to classroom- could not entirely escape the grip of that system. His degree- just like my mother's- should have elevated him. In many ways, it did. But the deep-seated caste system refused to let go.

In the hacienda, proximity to privilege meant everything. And skin tone became currency. Lighter skin suggested less labor, less sun- less poverty. It wasn't just beauty, it was class. The phrase "the whiter the better" wasn't just about color. It was code- a shorthand for who deserved respect and who didn't. House helpers weren't just indoors; they were, quite literally, in a whiter world.

Looking back, I see now that what shaped us was not just colonial hangover or casual colorism- it was something deeper and more insidious. It was the quiet fusion of racism and caste: two systems built to rank human worth. One focused on skin tone and racial features, the other on bloodlines, class, and inherited status. But both told us who belonged at the top, and who should stay silent, invisible, or ashamed. We didn't have the language for it then, but we felt it in the way lighter skin opened doors- and darker skin shut them. It wasn't just about beauty. It was about power.

After years of toiling under the unyielding sun, my father returned to his province as a man transformed- not only by education but by the scars of a system that prized labor over life. From a young boy uncertain of his future to a man assured of it. He stood a little taller, smiled a little longer. As a substitute teacher, he carried with him the memories of those fields, a quiet determination that spoke louder than any words could.

But mobility in the teaching profession came with its own set of challenges. The Department of Education, in its own way, perpetuated a system of class mobility that felt more like displacement. Teachers were assigned not necessarily where they were from, but where they were needed. My father, like many other substitute teachers, found himself moving from one school to another, never quite settling.

It was in one of those assignments that he met my mother. He was nervous about approaching her- they were total opposites in many ways. But as the saying goes, opposites attract.

He had escaped the hacienda, but not entirely. Its rules lived on in the unspoken gestures he carried: the lowered gaze, the careful silence, the reverence for education as a path to dignity. And in me- in the skin I did not choose, but love, in the comments I did not understand- we both lived with its echo.

Because even as we climbed, the ladder was crooked. And even after the sun had set on the fields he once worked, its light and its shadow remained.

But history doesn't just shape nations- it shapes dinner tables, back-yards, and even how we raise chickens.

Chapter 7: The House on the Hill, The Chicken in the Yard

"In the dew of little things, the heart finds its morning and is refreshed."
 -Kahlil Gibran

My mother was the kind of woman who walked into a room and instantly made it warmer. My father, on the other hand, could sit in that same room for hours, perfectly content with silence. She was all enthusiasm and motion; he was careful and deliberate. If she was the first to break the ice at social gatherings, he was the last to leave his seat. She sought out life; he let life come to him.

According to my mother, she first saw my father in the teacher's lounge of the school where they first met. She noticed how he kept mostly to himself and would steal a glance of her ever so often. She paid no attention to it until her co-teachers teased her about it. "Did you notice that guy staring at you? I think he likes you!", they would say. One of the teachers approached my father, "Do you want to talk to her? Go on, talk to her!", she egged him on. He finally found the courage to approach her.

Dating back then was very traditional. My mother told me that they always had a chaperon who went everywhere they went. The chaperon was usually a lady friend of my mother who would stay away from earshot to give the couple some privacy. It must have been awkward, I thought. My parents exchanged letters while dating and after almost a year, they decided to get married. My mother later told me that she chose dad as her lifetime partner when she saw how much he cared for her, how sincere he was in his words and actions. He was clean and industrious, traits that are important to my mother. He was also welcoming of my mother's large extended family and her friends.

Before they could get married, my dad had to ask my mother's father for her hand in marriage. My grandfather wasn't stern, but he had a dry sense of humor.

On the way to her parents' house, knowing that my father was so nervous, my mother coached him to be direct with her father before he lost his nerve. She told him to just wait for him to respond before saying anything else. So, he did as coached. My dad waited for my grandfather's response. What was probably only a minute seemed like forever, as he waited in agony, the room suddenly getting stifling hot. My grandfather finally smiled, gave my dad his blessing, then laughed out loud having noticed that my father was shaking in his boots.

"I have never seen your dad sweat so much! I thought he was going to faint!", my mom told us one time.

In my province, an engagement didn't require a ring- it required a pig. The groom-to-be had to provide a healthy pig for the bride's family, which would be butchered during the engagement party. The elders would then examine its bile, believing that its color foretold the couple's future. A yellowish-green bile was considered a sign of a strong and prosperous marriage.

From what I was told, no elder in either of my parents' families had ever declared a pig unhealthy.

Oftentimes during social gatherings, my mother would take the initiative to start a conversation with my father and other guests. It takes a bit for him to warm up but once he does, he can be a conversationalist. He also had a keen sense of humor! My mother's family are jokesters, and they would tease my dad for being so quiet. "Why are you so quiet? Did you do something that you are not telling us about?", one uncle would say. My father would blush and would tease back, "No, I just didn't want to take the spotlight away from you." Then they would join together in laughter. They loved him though. He supported my mother's decision to take on the responsibility to take care of her younger siblings, despite making so little as schoolteachers. Then of course there's us, their own children, to support.

When it came to parenting, my mother and father were always united in their decisions. A choice made by one was fully supported by the other, and we were never to play one against the other. But when it came to discipline, their approach was more nuanced- something my mother had intentionally set in place.

I remember one time when she was scolding me- I no longer recall what for. My father tried to chime in, but my mother gently stopped him and sent me away. Curious about what had just happened, I lingered within earshot. I overheard her quietly say, "You don't need to reprimand our children when I'm already doing it. Just as I won't reprimand them when you already are." My father simply nodded.

Later, my mother explained her reasoning. One parent, she believed, should always act as an ally to the child in trouble. No matter what

90

the mistake, a child should always feel they have someone to turn to for comfort and understanding.

My mother was the rock of our family. It seemed that she can always think on her feet so quickly to appease the worry that sometimes gets so heavy for my father. He was always worried about everything. He left school teaching to make more money in the insurance business, but it was a hard job. He was a traveling salesman, and he often had to travel outside of our province to sell insurance. We would know when it was a successful trip or not by his demeanor before he even walks in the door. He loved whistling a tune and he would do so when he's in a good mood. So, we would listen for that tune. We would know right away if the trip was a success. We would run up to him and start telling him how our days went while he was away. He would banter back, happy to be home.

It is a different atmosphere when the trip wasn't successful. He would be so deflated when he didn't land an account, he would walk in with a worried look on his face. We would see him shrink to a chair somewhere in the house. And my mother would be there cheering him on, telling him that everything would be alright. My siblings and I would not know what to say, so we would just walk away and leave our parents be. It was difficult to see him that way, but I didn't know how to cheer him up.

Though my father struggled with expressing his thoughts and feelings, his love for his family was undeniable. To support us, he travelled far and wide, rain or shine, as an insurance agent. To increase his income, he decided to open an office in the next province. It required him to be away from us once a month for several days. To cut down on travel time, he and my mother bought him a motorcycle. He rode that motorcycle through rugged terrain hours on end. He kept that routine for a few years.

Dad and his beloved motorcycle, circa 1980s

When he packed for these trips, he would ask me to help him. I'd watch as he carefully laid out his dress shirts and pants, showing me how to iron out every wrinkle with smooth, deliberate strokes. "Crisp and clean," he'd say, nodding with approval. He taught me how to fold clothes so neatly they looked like they had just come off the store shelf. It's a skill I still carry today- people are often surprised by how tidy my folds are! Sometimes I wonder where he learned it- maybe during his time in the hacienda, or while working at the funeral parlor where attention to detail mattered deeply.

He had a black typewriter with round, clacking keys used to write letters and contracts for his clients. It sat prominently on his desk like a badge of professionalism. He used it to teach us the basics of typing. I remember trying to type without looking at the letters- awkward at first, but over time, my fingers started to find their rhythm. It wasn't easy. I'm still not the fastest typist, and someone once teased me that I pound on a computer keyboard like I'm still using a typewriter. Maybe I am. There's something satisfying about the weight of each key stroke, something old-school and dependable, like him.

Looking back, those quiet lessons- the way he ironed his shirts, folded them just right, or taught us to type with focus and care- were his way of preparing us for life. He didn't say much, but his actions spoke volumes. His sacrifices were woven into the fabric of our daily lives, into every wrinkle pressed, every mile ridden, every night spent on a wooden bench far from home. I didn't fully grasp it then, but now I see it clearly. This was love, steady and enduring, without need for grand gestures or words.

I never heard him complain, but the arrangement clearly took a toll on him- physically, mentally, emotionally. You could see it in the way his shoulders slumped or in the quiet moments when his eyes gave away more than he ever said. We missed him terribly during those trips. Once, my mother took us to visit his new office. The town wasn't much bigger than ours, but for my father, it was a land of possibility. His office sat on the ground floor of a modest building and had the unmistakable scent of fresh paint and concrete dust. Like many homes and offices in our province, it had concrete walls and floors that felt cool and unforgiving under bare feet. The space was simple- just a table, a few chairs, and a long wooden bench that doubled as his bed. He shared a bathroom with the other tenants in the back of the house. They were quiet, respectful people. One of them kept tiny turtles as pets. My little sister would crouch beside their basin, fascinated by their slow, deliberate movements. Even in that sparse place, there was a sense of care and dignity.

One time in the early years of this arrangement, he didn't come home as expected and we didn't know what was happening. We didn't have a telephone in the house, so communication was through letters or telegrams for emergencies. We didn't receive a telegram. After the second day of his not coming home, my mother was visibly worried. She knew something must be wrong. It was unlike my dad to be away without a good reason. My mother piled us into a bus to go check on him.

Less than halfway to his office, my mother saw a motorcycle from afar coming towards us. Her instincts told her it was our father, so she asked the bus driver to pull over and flag the motorist. It was indeed my father. My siblings and I watched as our mother got off the bus and approached our father. He had his face covered with a bandana under his helmet. It was cold that day. He removed the bandana to talk to our mother. She was visibly shaken as she looked at him with such care and concern, his eyes were bloodshot, and his lips cracked. He had been sick for the last few days. It shook us to see him that way. He looked frail and weak. Public display of affection is not the norm with our parents. Mostly because our culture wasn't into that, but also, I think it was the time- people were a lot more conservative in those days. But they loved and respected each other. There was never a cross word exchanged between the two of them and never did one talk badly of the other to us, their children, or to other people.

We somehow managed to get home together and our mother nursed him back to good health. We tried to be useful by helping with whatever mom needed to care, boiling water for his sponge bath, helping make dinner and being quiet to let him sleep his way back to being 100%. After a few days, he was back to normal and went about his daily mode of operation to take care of his family.

This experience made us realize how integral our father was to our lives. He may not be the life of the party, but he carried our lives on his shoulders. This experience also left an indelible mark in our memory. My sister told me not too long ago that our father's face, in that moment in time when he pulled down his bandana, is forever chiseled in her consciousness. She told me that she feels profound sadness each time she remembers that moment. That moment, when sacrifice had a face, and it was our father's.

My mother's faith was unshakable. She often said, "When God closes a door, He opens a window", though it wasn't always clear where that window was. She taught us to trust that even in our hardest moments, there was a plan unfolding. It was a little different with my father. His quiet nature often hid a well of worry that weighed on him like stones in his pockets. I remember how my mother would sit beside him, her hand on his shoulder, saying, "We'll find a way, as we always do."

FAITH AS SURVIVAL

My mother's faith was rooted in Christianity, specifically Catholicism, but it wasn't the religion she was born into. Her ancestor's belief is a complex system of animism, ancestor worship, and polytheism. They believed in numerous deities associated with nature and the different realms of the universe. Great importance is also placed on honoring ancestors, who are believed to be able to influence the lives of the living. These beliefs were manifested in rituals performed by specialized priests to appease deities and seek blessings for good health, harvest, and other aspects of life. My mother's family transitioned from Indigenous beliefs through education and colonial influence. Though they have become monotheists, they still observed some of the traditional practices like honoring one's ancestors and the environment.

Christianity was brought by Spanish missionaries and settlers in the 16th century, with the first recorded conversion in April 1521. Within 25 years of the first conversion, about a quarter million Filipinos- half of the population of the country at that time- converted to Christianity. This rapid rise was aided by books on catechism published by monastic presses in both Spanish and Tagalog- the precursor to the now Filipino language. Today, Christianity is still the predominant religion with 85.3% of the population, 78.8% Catholicism and 6.5% other Christian religions. Islam has 6.4% and the 8.2% are various religions or no religious affiliation.

For my mother, faith was not just a belief- it was survival. It was what kept her steady when my father worried and what kept food on our table when there seemed to be no way forward. She never doubted that God would provide. My father, however, found it harder to believe. He carried his worries heavily, while my mother carried them lightly, handing them over to God like an old friend she trusted completely.

SUNDAY MASS AND SWEET REWARDS

As a family we observed Sunday Mass, and all the other holiday and non-holiday obligations. As young children, my siblings and I relished Sundays, not for the mass itself but for what we received, occasionally, after church.

Money was always scarce, but I do not remember a time when there was no food at the table. Somehow, we were fed. Mother was also keen about eating healthy, which she learned from the Dutch nuns. We didn't have any fun food in the house though, like chips and soda. Probably a good thing since we couldn't afford them anyway. The only time she would indulge us is on some occasional Sundays after church at Mila's Canteen and Bakery.

The walk to Mila's Canteen after Sunday Mass was filled with anticipation. Even though the walk is only a few yards from church, it sure felt like forever as we impatiently composed ourselves and tried not to run to the canteen. The scent of freshly baked bread drifted through the air long before we arrived. Inside, the counters gleamed with rows of fluffy cakes, golden rolls, and pastel-colored icing. The angel cake was soft and sweet, melting on our tongues like a little piece of heaven. For a child, a slice of cake and a cold Coca-Cola were enough to make the world feel abundant. Those Sundays were brief escapes from the scarcity of everyday life, moments where we felt like royalty in a humble bakery.

THE TEACHER'S QUARTERS: A SHARED EXISTENCE

I had lofty dreams for someone born in a poor town in a third world country, where you are either born into wealth or you must work hard just to get by. I have watched my parents struggle to put food on the table. My mother, the second of 12 children, was orphaned early in her adult life so her unmarried siblings are also now dependent on her. I am the oldest of 4 so there were many people in our household relying on the wages of my parents who were schoolteachers.

Schoolteachers were paid so cheaply they weren't able to afford to have their own houses, so they lived in the quarters provided by the school system. The teachers' quarters felt more like a collage of lives stitched together than separate homes. Every sound, every word, and every argument seeped through the thin walls, becoming part of the rhythm of our days. At night, the rain drummed on the roof like a marching band, making it impossible to ignore the storms outside. Sometimes, my siblings and I would huddle together under a single blanket, pretending to be explorers in a jungle, as the rain and wind howled around us. It was a way to make the discomfort of those nights feel like an adventure. During the day, we would play hide and seek to distract ourselves. Some of the other children would join us so that the whole Quarters became a hiding place! The adults sometimes got annoyed by it, they couldn't wait for the sun to be back out so they could send us all out of the house!

As a child, I didn't mind being around so many people. However, I was impatient when in line to use the common areas, like the bathroom or the water sink. "Be patient," my mother reminded me often. Patiently waiting in line as a lesson didn't stick. To this day, without even realizing it, I would go straight to the front of the line, "Excuse me, there's a line," someone would inevitably say. "Oh, I'm sorry," I would say, slightly embarrassed as I make my way to the back of the line. I guess I am just a woman with a singular purpose!

The bedrooms smelled musty- lived in. But what unsettled me most was the feeling of being wet and cold at the same time. When the roof leaked and the rain ended up dripping on us, on our blanket, we would move to another part of the room, hoping that the leak stays on the other side of the room.

FINDING HOME: OUR FIRST HOME

Living in these squalid quarters, I watched my parents struggle daily-whether it was putting food on the table or clothes on our backs, every step was an uphill battle. I realized early on that I had to succeed, not just for myself but for them and the rest of our family. It was a tradition I witnessed firsthand through my mother's sacrifices: the oldest child in the family- or the second oldest, in her case- shouldered the responsibility of helping everyone else. It was the only way life could improve for all of us.

My parents eventually were able to buy a piece of land. They told us that they have scraped and saved any extra to be able to do that. I don't know how they did it because it seemed like there never was any extra. There was always just enough to feed the family, always just enough to afford a new pair of slippers. Always just enough. But I was ecstatic to hear that we were building our own house!

The land was carved into the slope of a hill, reachable only by foot. My parents had one side of the slope bulldozed and flattened to make space for the house; while leaving the other side intact- it functioned as a natural windbreak and offered a breathtaking view of the valleys below and the jagged silhouettes of mountains beyond. The dirt road didn't quite reach the property, so my parents cleared shrubs and small trees to extend it to a narrow footpath. Even then, vehicles couldn't make the final climb. We'd get off the jeepneys at the base of the hill, the engine wheezing in protest, and hike the rest of the way. The path was steep and uneven, often slick with mud after a downpour. Our shoes kicked up dust in the dry season, and the scent of crushed grass and wild guava leaves perfumed the air. Bamboo stalks creaked gently in the breeze, and the chorus of cicadas rose and fell with the heat, as if the hillside itself were exhaling.

I loved walking the other side of the slope, where it opened up into silence and sky. Up there, the small-town noise fell away, replaced by the rustle of leaves and the distant sound of roosters crowing in unseen farms. It was quiet in a way that felt sacred. I would pause sometimes, just to take it all in- the sweep of green below, the soft clouds catching on mountaintops, the warmth of the sun on my back. It felt like the world had cracked open, just for me.

And then I'd turn and head back down, toward the little house we were building- not much more than concrete floors and corrugated roofing, but standing bravely on its patch of earth, our first real stake in the world. The contrast between that quiet, expansive view and the modest shelter below reminded me: we didn't have much, but we had a place to belong.

That house was small and basic, no insulation, no ceiling- just a roof- and no indoor plumbing. Gas was expensive so my parents built an outdoor wood-fired kitchen to keep smoke from permeating the house. The bathrooms were also outside of the house. Simple as it was, it became the axis of my understanding of home- not defined by luxury, but by the roots we laid down, the sky above us, and the way the wind moved through the trees. It taught me that security isn't always about what you can hold in your hands, but what holds you- quiet hills, shared dreams, the certainty that you have a place to return to. And even now, years and oceans away, when the world feels too loud or unsure, I still think of that hill. That narrow footpath. That house. And I remember: we built something. We belonged somewhere. We still do.

It may have been humble, but it was a significant improvement from the Teachers Quarters. We had privacy, and it wasn't loud and noisy from the other families. The first night was so quiet, we could hear the crickets and the frogs. The soft rustling of the tree leaves sounded like a lullaby. It made our first night peaceful. My siblings and I felt like we were finally home.

And though the house may have changed, or the trees have grown taller, the memory of that first quiet night remains, untouched, unshaken, mine.

CREATING PARADISE: THE LAND OF ORCHIDS

The house sat on a piece of land that felt like paradise to us. The plateau offered a stunning view of the mountains, where the sunrise painted the sky in hues of orange and pink. My mother transformed the patch of land into her canvas, growing fruits like banana, papaya, pineapple, and planting rows of vegetables, grafting wild orchids onto the branches of a towering tree in front of our home. Each orchid, she told us, was a gift from the forest, a reminder that even in the hardest circumstances, beauty could bloom. She used to stand beneath the tree and marvel at how beautiful it looked with all the different colors from the orchids. "Nature is full of wonders." She would tell us. My father would walk up to the hill behind the house and look around,

101

loving the 360 views around him, smiling with quiet satisfaction. He must have thought that he accomplished something. And he did.

Hunting for wild orchids in the lush forests was one of our greatest adventures. The air was thick with the scent of damp earth and leaves, and the forest was alive with the hum of insects and the occasional rustle of unseen animals. We'd scramble over rocks and through undergrowth, competing to see who could find the most vibrant orchid for our mother. Bringing her the orchids felt like a small triumph, a way of saying, "Look what we found for you!" And when she grafted them onto the tree, it felt as though a part of the forest had come home with us.

Our home overflowed not just with chores and stories, but with music. Our mother loved Anne Murray's gentle melodies, while our father played Engelbert Humperdinck and Gary Lewis & the Playboys. Of the two, he was the dancer. He taught us the cha-cha and the waltz, lifting my sister and me onto his feet, guiding us through the steps until we could dance on our own. It wasn't just fun- it was a kind of bonding, the rhythm of love in motion between father and child.

That home held more than music and movement- it became the backdrop of some of our most treasured childhood memories, especially around Christmas time.

OUR FIRST REAL CHRISTMAS

It was also in our new home that we finally had our first real Christmas tree, and our first Christmas presents under the tree on Christmas morning. Living with other families in the Teacher's Quarters had made it tricky to have either. First, any decision about a tree had to be made by the group. Second, there was always the risk of theft. And third- my mother's ever-present sensitivity- she didn't want the other families, especially the children, to feel bad if they had no gifts.

The Christmas tree we had wasn't spruce or pine- those didn't grow in our province. Instead, it was more like a version of Charlie Brown's tree, just with more branches. Still, we were thrilled! Just as we made most things by hands, we made homemade Christmas ornaments by tracing shapes from our books- snowflakes, bells, snowmen, and stars- then cutting them out and threading them with sewing machine thread to hang on the tree. "This is so much fun!" Bugsy exclaimed through her missing front teeth- she was barely five years old at the time.

On Christmas morning, we all woke up early to see what Santa brought us. Bugsy found a ball tucked into the hood of her sweater. Little Chris got a toy car, but I don't remember what Jun, and I received. What I do remember vividly is the feeling of cold coins under my feet as I stepped toward the tree. Our parents had scattered one-peso coins on the floor underneath it! I squealed with excitement, scooping up coins, until I heard one of my uncles' shouts, "There are 20-peso bills hanging on the tree!" I switched gears and began hunting for more bills.

There weren't any more twenties, just tens and fives- but I still ended up with 25 pesos! That might have only been about a US dollar, but I was over the moon. Up to that point, I'd never had more than a peso on me, ever! That following Saturday, I went to the market with my parents and bought my first pink girly purse- it cost 10 pesos. I tucked the rest of my loot inside. I didn't spend another centavo for months; I just liked the feeling of having a little money.

It was the best Christmas memory of my childhood. To this day, each Christmas morning, I think back to that moment- Santa really came through for us that year. Years later, Bugsy told me how proud she had been telling her friends, "Santa brought me a ball!" only for them to laugh and say, "There's no Santa, silly!" That was when she first began to doubt. I told her I already knew there was no Santa Claus even then-, but I believed in St. Nicholas. We laugh about it now, and marvel at how much Christmas has changed, how commercialized it has become.

Those small joys- the tree, the coins, the homemade decorations- made our new home feel magical. But the magic didn't end with the holidays. Everyday life, with all its quirks and routines, offered its own kind of joy... and its fair share of chores.

We also had some chickens and a couple of pigs in the back. We helped feed them, the chickens with grains and the pigs with whatever vegetables, mostly cabbage and yams, that my mother would boil. I preferred feeding the chickens, the pigs were, well, pigs. My siblings and I would gather the eggs from the chickens and help clean the coops and pig pen. I didn't like that part much. The smell, ugh! Chicken dungs are the worst! For such small creatures, their dung stank to high heavens!

As the holidays passed, the daily rhythms of home life returned, filled with chores, laughter, and the occasional whiff of chicken dung.

THE CHOSEN CHICKEN: A LESSON IN PURPOSE

We did have our pick of our own chicken for our birthdays. The process of raising a chicken for a birthday feast was both simple and profound. As children we didn't think much about it. We'd pick a scrawny chick, name it, and then watch it grow fat under our care. But as I grew older, I began to see the deeper truth: every creature has a purpose. Some are destined to give, like the hens laying eggs, while others are destined to sacrifice.

I remember one particular birthday when I had chosen a small, scrappy chick months before. I had named it Puti, for its pale-yellow feathers, and each morning, I scattered grains for it, watching as it darted between the bigger chickens, always quick and clever enough to get its share. It grew into a plump, beautiful bird, its white feathers catching the sunlight as it strutted around the yard. When my birthday approached, my mother reminded me that it was time to prepare Puti.

I hesitated. For the first time, I saw more than just a meal- I saw something I had raised, something that had trusted me. It had pecked grain from my palm, followed me around the yard, and nestled into the coop at night without fear. How could it possibly understand what was coming?

I asked my mother if we could pick a different chicken, maybe one of the others that I hadn't fed by hand. She gave me a knowing look, her voice gentle but firm. "Puti was chosen for a reason," she said. "Just like we all have our part in this life." I didn't resist after that. Somehow, I understood, but I was still sad.

That night, as we gathered around the table, I took a bite of the tender, fragrant meat. It was the same comforting taste I had known all my life, yet something felt different. I chewed slowly, the weight of understanding settling deep in my chest. Still, I felt lucky to be able to enjoy such a meal.

Sometimes I think about those chickens and all the chores we did for them- not just because they fed us or laid eggs, but because they remind me of a different kind of richness. In a life that didn't offer much in the way of luxuries, we still had so much: music, laughter, love, and even a Christmas tree strung with paper ornaments and dreams.

The chosen chicken wasn't just the one set aside for a feast or a special occasion. In a way, we were all chosen, chosen to carry forward what our parents gave us: a life of meaning shaped by humility, resilience, and joy in simple things. That tree, that purse, those coins underfoot, even the stinky chicken dung- they're all part of the same memory collage. A time when we had little but felt full. A time when a pink purse could make you feel rich, and a chicken in the yard could remind you that you belonged to something bigger than yourself.

For the first time, I wondered about my own role in the world. Was I meant to be like the hens, giving endlessly, always replenishing? Or was I like Puti-nurtured for a time, only to be taken for a greater purpose?

I never found a definitive answer to that question- not then, and not even now. But I've come to understand that the asking itself matters. In every season of my life- through struggle, sacrifice, joy, and doubt- I keep circling back to that same wondering: what is my part in all this? Am I meant to give endlessly, or was I nurtured for a purpose larger than I can yet grasp?

In moments of quiet reflection, I think of Shakespeare's words:

"Nothing is so common as the wish to be remarkable." That longing- to matter, to make a difference- is something I still carry. Perhaps it's not about finding a clear role, but about becoming someone who honors the life she's been given, who keeps striving, searching, and growing- even when the path ahead is uncertain.

That's where I came from. A place where coins on the floor could feel like gold, and a pink purse could carry a girl's entire world. Not just a chosen chicken, but a life that has been forged by fire- and still full of hope.

Looking back, that little house on the hill was more than shelter- it was our first glimpse of what it meant to shape a life with our own hands. Every tree we planted, every egg we gathered, every ornament we strung was a quiet act of becoming. We were no longer just surviving; we were creating something. A home. A rhythm. A sense of purpose.

At the time, I didn't yet have the words for it. But something in me was shifting- growing more aware that even the smallest tasks carried meaning. That a life, like a house, could be built with care, sacrifice, and joy. It would take time before I understood just how deeply that truth would shape me- how even a chicken in the yard could open a door to the questions that would follow me for years.

Chapter 8: Walis and Wisdom, Jeepneys and Motorcycles

"The only way to make sense out of change is to plunge into it, move with it, and join the dance."
 - Alan Watts

The jump from elementary to high school felt like being thrown into a different world. It wasn't just the academic workload- it was the sudden shift in how I saw myself, how I was seen by others, and how I now had to navigate new social rules. Every hallway felt unfamiliar, and every classmate, an unknown figure in my own story.

I started high school when I was just twelve years old. In the Philippines at that time, there was no middle school system- students went directly from 6th grade in elementary school to their freshman year of high school. Most students graduate high school at 16, becoming college freshmen at the same age, or sometimes even younger. The first day of school was a little intimidating. It was in a different town, and I didn't know most of the students. The walls were concrete, and chairs were uncomfortable. I kept to myself the first day, but after a few days, I felt at ease and started interacting with my classmates. It also helped that one of the students was a neighbor back home, so I had somebody familiar.

Although my parents couldn't afford the tuition, they wanted me to attend the school, so they submitted my grades for scholarship consideration. I was awarded a scholarship! The look on my parents' faces when they found out- joy mixed with relief- was priceless. My mother, always so selfless in making sure we had what we needed, and my father, whose quiet pride was evident in everything he did, had given everything they could just to get me into this school. That scholarship wasn't just about grades- it was their dream, too. It also opened a door- not just to a school with a sturdy reputation, but to a new world of traditions, expectations, and opportunities. It was also a big load off their shoulders, and I was excited to attend a good school. With my scholarship secured, I was now officially part of a school known for its rigorous academics and deep-rooted Catholic traditions.

I was fortunate to attend the Catholic high school. The school is a private Catholic basic education institution that caters to all students in town and nearby towns in the province. It was founded by a Dutch missionary and then was run by nuns and priests of the CICM order. By the time I was a student in the school, most of the teachers were lay people with a few nuns teaching music and religion. We still were required to uphold the tradition of the Catholic school; for example, we were to attend mass for the first Friday of the month, and the Month of the Rosary, and all the other major Christian Holidays like Christmas and Easter.

It was a bit rigid, but at that time and place, they offered the best option for quality education. I didn't mind the rigidity much because I didn't know any better. I grew up practicing what the school required, so it was no big deal. We also wore uniforms- white blouses and blue pleated skirts for girls, white shirts, and blue pants for boys. There was nothing fashionable about them, but I was thankful. I didn't have many nice civilian clothes, and in a way, the uniform was a kind of equalizer. School life had its routines, and the campus itself became a kind of second home.

The school campus sat in one of the loveliest parts of town. The grounds were always well kept, with bright Bermuda grass covering the quadrangle where students lingered during free periods. That patch of green- prickly on the skin- became my favorite part of the campus, so we'd spread our sweaters or towels to sit on. I spent countless hours there with friends, sprawled on the grass, talking about class, boys, and our dreams for the future.

The school building itself was a stark, three-story structure made of concrete and wood. Though I learned a lot inside, it was my least favorite part of the campus. It could get really cold during the colder months. There was no heating system, so we had to bundle up in jackets and scarves, even inside the classroom.

The gymnasium hosted the biggest events- graduations, contests, and all the extracurriculars that didn't involve sports. For those, we had a concrete basketball court and a wide-open field.

But the center of everything was the church and the convent. The church felt cold, too, with its stone floors and tall, echoing ceilings. Still, it was where everyone went for school Masses, town Masses, holy days.

The First Friday Masses were a source of endless amusement for me and my friends. Sister Maria, who was Dutch and very proper, sang in a high falsetto that we could never quite get used to. We'd try to hold in our giggles whenever she hit a particularly sharp note, hiding behind our hymnals like that would help. But Sister Maria had eyes like a hawk. The moment she shot us one of her famous glares- chin tilted, lips pursed, eyes sharp as needles- we'd sit up straight and pretend we were deep in prayer.

The kneelers didn't help either. They weren't padded, and I'd fidget on my bony knees, shifting from side to side. That always earned me another look. She never said a word about it- just that look.

But outside of Mass, Sister Maria was surprisingly kind. She always greeted us when we passed her in the hallways, and she never mentioned our giggling fits in church. Once, I asked her where she was going, just trying to make conversation. She answered politely, then gently told me that in her culture, that kind of question could be considered intrusive. It wasn't harsh- just matter of fact. But it stayed with me. It was the first time I realized that some questions shouldn't be asked unless the relationship allows for it. That small moment taught me more about respect than any lesson in class.

I didn't think much about faith then. But even with all the discomfort and the stifled laughter, there was always a feeling when I stepped inside that space. A kind of hush. Like something important could happen there.

Looking back, I see how those years quietly shaped my idea of faith- not just the kind taught in religion class or practiced at Mass, but the kind that shows up in discipline, in sacrifice, in showing up every day even when it's hard. At the time, I was just living it, not naming it. But it stayed with me.

The school was more than an hour away by public transportation, and the daily commute was no small feat. For many of us from small towns like mine, the norm was to stay with family friends or distant relatives during the school week, returning home on weekends. If no such arrangement could be made, students would often rent a small room in someone's home near the school- whatever it took to get an education.

During my freshman year, I stayed with a family friend who had children attending the same high school. It was a blessing to have familiar faces around me and friends to walk with to school. Each school day settled into a rhythm- walks to school, shared meals, and small discoveries like the abundance of avocado trees that lined our path, offering both shade and surprise. Their branches were heavy with fruit, and many avocados would fall to the roadside. I often found a ripe one, checked it for bruises, peeled off the skin, and ate it like a banana as I walked. These days, I cut them in half like most people. Sometimes I think about eating one the old way again, but I never quite do.

Not all interactions during those walks were kind, though. One encounter sticks out clearly. A girl in the neighborhood started yelling my name for no reason I can remember. "Jane, I'm going to hurt you! You better watch out!" At first, I was surprised, and I wondered why. The second time, I was a bit nervous, and I was going to answer her. "Don't," said one of my family friends," Just ignore her. She'll get tired of it soon enough." She was right. After a few more times of her yelling and my ignoring her, she finally stopped. We became friendly much later in the year and I never asked why she did what she did. But I still wonder, would my answering her possibly have worsened the situation? Would she have actually hurt me? I would never know, but that incident stayed fresh in my memory. That was my first experience with bullying, and I didn't get bullied much after that.

Looking back now, I sometimes wonder how I wasn't bullied more often. I was studious-definitely a "nerd" by most standards- but I wasn't shy or withdrawn. I made friends easily, laughed often, and enjoyed being part of things. Still, by the usual playground logic, I should have been an easy target. I was lucky. Maybe my energy or confidence threw people off. Whatever the reason, I was spared more of it, and for that, I'm grateful.

But my heart aches for those who weren't as fortunate- for the ones who walked into school every day with a knot in their stomachs, who were mocked, ignored, or made to feel small. No one deserves that.

That brief encounter taught me something I couldn't have understood then: that cruelty often comes from pain, and silence isn't always weakness- it can be strategy, even strength. I didn't confront her, not because I was afraid, but because something in me understood that not reacting might be the safest path. And it worked. She moved on, and eventually, so did I.

Still, the experience stayed with me. It shaped how I show up for others- how I notice who feels out of place, how I listen more closely, how I offer kindness without being asked. Not because I'm a saint, but because I know what it's like to be targeted... even if just for a moment.

My mother always told us to lead with grace. "You don't have to fight every battle," she'd say, "especially if it costs you your peace." At the time, I didn't understand how wisdom could sound so much like surrender. But now I do. There's power in restraint, dignity in choosing when- and whether- to respond. Sometimes, staying grounded is the bravest thing you can do.

And sometimes, bravery looks like peeling an avocado with your bare hands and eating it whole while walking to school- completely unfazed, juice dripping down your wrist, classmates looking at you like you're slightly unhinged. But hey, I was hungry. And it was ripe.

Those small rituals- the quiet resistance to cruelty, the soft laughter between friends, the simple joy of an unexpected snack- carried me through that year. Also, the responsibilities of living away from home was made lighter by the kindness of the family who took me in. Their generosity made the transition easier. I poured myself into my studies, fueled by curiosity, determination, and perhaps a little bit of avocado oil. When I ranked first in my freshman class, I didn't feel triumphant- I felt steady. Like maybe I was beginning to understand who I was becoming. It also wasn't something I expected, but it affirmed what my mother always told me- that no matter where I came from, I could rise above it.

I did feel proud of getting first place; it validated my scholarship and gave my confidence a significant boost. As a freshman, you're still finding your footing, and I had found mine. I wasn't just another student- I had made an early mark. I think my classmates saw me a little differently too, perhaps with admiration, envy, or a mix of both. My parents were at the awards ceremony, and you could see the pride radiating from their faces. My father's smile was so wide it looked like it might split his face in two, and my mother kept clasping her hands together in front of her chest, her eyes glistening with joy. You couldn't wipe the smiles off their faces- especially my father's.

As we left the ceremony, teachers and other parents stopped to congratulate them. Each time, my father puffed up a little more, proudly announcing, "My daughter took first honor!" He must have repeated it to half a dozen people on the way out. My mother, ever the gracious one, gently nudged him and said, "Okay na, that's enough," but the glow on his face didn't fade.

That moment stayed with me- not just because of the award, but because I saw myself through their eyes. In that brief walk out of the school, I wasn't just a student. I was their daughter. And in their eyes, I was enough.

By my sophomore year, my younger brother Jun joined me at high school as a freshman. To accommodate both of us, my parents rented a couple of rooms in a boarding house near the school, creating a new routine for our weekday lives.

Boarding houses in the Philippines are similar to rooming houses in the United States. You have your own private room but share all the common areas, including the kitchen and bathroom. Our rooms were cramped but the shared areas were spacious. The first floor had a receiving area with a large hand carved wooden statue of a man depicting a triumphant man from battle. His face had the look of victory, his left arm raised above holding a severed head and his right arm hung by his side holding a bolo, a machete-like weapon. He was wearing nothing more than a wanoh- a traditional loincloth for Ifugao men. My friends and I would sometimes jokingly push it aside to reveal a life size male member, and we would sneak away when the elderly couple who owned the house yelled at us to stop.

We were the only students there, which made me feel both independent and strangely isolated. The couple was kind but distant, and I remember the quietness of the house sometimes being overwhelming. It was as if time moved slower in that space- a stark contrast to the chaos of my daily life. They were also kind and eccentric. The husband was a retired lawyer, but I don't recall what the wife did for work. They both loved talking about their son, who was also a lawyer and lived in the big city. One day, I noticed the wife quietly opening and closing closets after the husband left the house. Curious, I followed her quietly. "A-ha!", I heard her say suddenly. I peeked from behind the door of the closet and found her pinching one side of her mouth as she stuck the bottle of gin on the other side of her mouth and started chugging. I looked at her with probably an incredulous look on my face, she looked at me and spoke. "Promise me you won't say anything to anybody!"

I never said anything to her husband. I also did not understand what I saw. Years later, I believe it was her coping mechanism for being bored- she wasn't doing much of anything, she was always home. Perhaps, she was even an alcoholic. And if she was, I never saw her personality shift; she was almost always quiet and kept to herself. And yet all my memories of her and her husband are of gratitude. They didn't need to rent us rooms, but they did. They were kind to us and even shared their food with us when we were lacking. Sometimes the water was intermittent, and the toilets clogged, but that was common everywhere. I think back to those years in their house with a smile and deep gratitude.

Unlike rooming houses, where meals are included in the cost, boarding houses in the Philippines only provide a place to stay- no meals are provided. This meant my brother and I had to cook for us, and it was an education of its own- one that left its mark, quite literally.

One time, I was distracted while cooking rice- maybe lost in thought or caught up in something else. Suddenly, I heard the boiling water hissing and spilling over the pot. I rushed to lift the lid, but the steam shot out, searing my wrist. I yelped, dropping the cover with a clatter and nearly tipping the pot over. I bolted to the sink, thrusting my arm under cool water as a deep, throbbing pain settled in. The skin turned an angry red, but I knew it could have been worse.

That burn left a scar- oddly shaped like a figure eight- etched into my right wrist like a permanent reminder. It faded with time eventually but for a while, reminders were constant. Whenever I reached for something, there it was. Whenever I cooked, whenever I washed dishes, it stared back at me, making sure I never made the same mistake again.

We were also required to help clean the boarding house, especially the common areas, which involved mostly sweeping dirt and dust. There was no vacuum cleaner, so we swept the floors with a walis tambo- a type of soft, handheld broom, traditionally made from the flower stalks of the Phragmite reed. Walis means to sweep and tambo refers to the Phragmite reed. Walis tambo is crafted by bundling the flower stalks, drying them and then forming the soft, whisk-like bristles. For the yard, we used the walis tingting, another type of broom made from dried palm leaves and is typically used for sweeping outdoors, like the yard.

At barely thirteen, I was already responsible for cooking, cleaning, and taking care of my younger brother. There was no one to swoop in if I made a mistake. At times, especially when I saw my classmates gallivanting while I was doing my chores, I felt envious. I longed to join them. But I found a way to make it work- by learning to prioritize my responsibilities. I would finish my homework in class, which gave me the chance to join them after school before heading home. I don't think I ever felt lonely, not only because I had so much to do, but also because I wasn't the only one in the same situation. That made it easier to cope.

I had to learn- sometimes the hard way. But with each mishap, I became more capable. More cautious. More independent. The burn eventually faded, but the scar stayed. And so did the lesson: pay attention, stay present, and take responsibility- even for the smallest things, like a pot of rice.

Every weekday morning, we would get up and start the day with breakfast, pack our lunch then get ready for school. We come back at the end of the day, do whatever chores needed to be done. We would then cook dinner, eat, do our homework then go to bed. The following morning, we would wake up and do it over again. We cooked very basic food, like rice, eggs, vegetables, and the occasional meat. We would wash our own dishes and save our soiled clothes, which we took home with us every weekend.

Beyond our little boarding house, the chaos of daily commuting awaited. It meant more than just learning independence- it also meant navigating the daily chaos of public transportation.

We walked to and from school every day. On rare occasions when we could afford it, we flagged a tricycle- our version of a taxi. A tricycle is essentially a motorcycle with a covered sidecar, and a roof that extends to shield both the sidecar and the driver. It could squeeze in five people: the driver, one passenger riding pillion behind him, another wedged in the narrow gap between the sidecar and the motorcycle-sitting sideways with his back to the driver- and two more on the main seat inside the sidecar. Most of the time, there'd be a sixth passenger hanging off the side of the sidecar, gripping the frame as we bumped along the road.

Every Sunday afternoon, we would leave home, take a jeepney to the neighboring town where our boarding house was, and settle in for the school week. From Monday to Friday, we followed this routine, and on Friday afternoons, we'd ride a jeepney back home to spend the weekend with our family.

Jeepney rides weren't just about enduring the crowd; they were also an immersion into the vibrant street life of the Philippines. Vendors would hop on at various stops, weaving their way through the packed passengers, selling everything from bottled water to roasted peanuts, and, of course, balut or penoy. The smell of the warm, broth-filled delicacy would waft through the vehicle as a vendor called out, "Baluuuut! Peeenoy!" Some passengers would eagerly dig into the steaming eggs, cracking them open with practiced ease, sprinkling salt or drizzling vinegar over the developing duck embryo before slurping it down.

It might be unappetizing for foreigners, but for locals, balut and penoy were a childhood staple, something eaten on cool evenings or after a long day. But for foreigners, it was often treated as a dare, a test of bravery that separated the adventurous from the squeamish. We had all seen a tourist go pale at the sight of the partially formed chick inside, hesitant to take that first bite while locals egged them on- pun intended. "Kaya mo yan!" (You can do it!) someone would always say with a laugh.

Meanwhile, as the vendor made his way down the aisle, the jeepney driver, barely turning his head, would bark the inevitable command: "Siksikan pa! Walang malalaglag!" (Move in tighter! No one should fall out!) Passengers shuffled closer, squeezing together like sardines, making just enough room for one more person. As the vendor hopped off at the next stop, the jeepney lurched forward again, cramming even more passengers inside. I adjusted my grip on the overhead bar, bracing myself for the sudden jerks and turns. This routine- squeezing into packed vehicles, brushing shoulders with strangers, and watching life unfold in quick snapshots through the open windows- was just part of getting to and from school.

But on rare occasions, Jun and I got to skip the chaos of public transport altogether. Instead of cramming into a jeepney, we'd get to ride with our father on his motorcycle.

Riding on my father's motorcycle was one of my favorite memories. When I was younger, his motorcycle seemed like an extension of him-like a silent partner in everything he did. He polished it obsessively, his pride shining through every gleam of chrome. It was more than just a mode of transportation; it was his escape, his joy, and to him, it represented freedom- something he treasured deeply after years of arduous work. I remember how, despite the teasing from my mother about how much time he spent cleaning the bike, my dad never seemed to mind. To him, it was never about the dirt- it was about the thrill of the open road and the adventures that awaited him just beyond the horizon.

When Jun and I were allowed to ride along, it felt like we were part of that adventure. Sometimes, we would stand by the roadside, eagerly awaiting his return from the day's work, and we'd race to him when we heard that unmistakable roar of his engine. As he pulled up, we'd pile onto the seat behind him, squeezing as close as we could to each other to fit, the wind rushing past us. And when my father would give a playful warning to hold on tight, it only made the moment feel more exhilarating.

On clear days, the rides were pure joy. We'd wind our way through the mountains, the cool breeze cutting through the heat of the day, the hum of the engine filling the air. We leaned into the sharp turns, feeling the pull of gravity as we curved with the bike. My dad's hands on the throttle, steady and experienced, gave me a sense of safety I will never forget.

But on rainy days, the same rides took on a different mood. The droplets stung against my skin, and the world around us blurred as the rain hammered against our faces. My brother and I would huddle close, trying to shield ourselves as much as possible, but the thrill was still there - mixed with the coolness of the rain and the rush of the ride. Even then, we knew that a day like this wasn't the same as a perfect ride, but it still held a unique kind of beauty.

Looking back, the motorcycle wasn't just a bike- it was a reflection of my father's resilience and his way of showing love. It was through those rides, in the shared quiet of the road, that I began to see my father not just as a provider, but as a man with hopes, dreams, and his own story of survival. I realize now that those moments on the motorcycle were more than just adventures- they were the quiet, unspoken bond between us. And for me, those rides became more than just a way to get from one place to another; they were an experience- one that connected me to my father in a way nothing else did. The motorcycle wasn't just his escape. It became our shared adventure, one that remains a vivid, cherished memory in my mind. No matter how uncomfortable some of the rides were, they were always worth it- a reminder that even the simplest moments could be the ones that stayed with us forever.

That summer, my high school hosted a neighborhood basketball league, and to no one's surprise, my father was a regular fixture in the audience. He loved basketball. I mean, absolutely loved it- with the quiet, unwavering loyalty he reserved for the things that brought him joy. He knew the players' names, their stats, even their shooting patterns. He had no formal training in the sport, but he watched with such intensity you'd think he had coached a national team.

It wasn't long before the game announcers- who were more like barkers with a megaphone-noticed his enthusiasm. "Tay, try mo nga!" they teased one afternoon, handing him the mic. He looked startled at first, as if he couldn't quite believe the offer was real. But then, with a chuckle and a scratch of his head, he took the mic and cleared his throat.

His commentary was rough around the edges- he fumbled a few names, got a bit too excited during a fast break, and once even forgot to speak for an entire play- but the crowd loved him. His voice, hesitant but genuine, floated over the court like a warm breeze. Each time he stumbled, he would scratch his head and laugh, the mic catching the soft chuckle before he found his footing again. You could hear the affection in the laughter that followed his every slip-up. He wasn't polished, but he was beloved. In that moment, he wasn't just a father or a teacher- he was part of the game.

I remember sitting in the stands, watching him, a quiet smile on my face. He looked so happy. And it made me proud. It was a side of him that most people didn't often see- joyful, lighthearted, taking up space.

It's a small memory, maybe. But when I think back on those days, that one sticks. Before life got complicated. Before I started asking questions I wasn't ready to answer. Before the weight of growing up settled on my shoulders. There was my father, awkwardly clutching a microphone, mispronouncing a player's name, and beaming like he'd just won the championship himself.

To this day, every time I watch an NBA game, I think of him. Not just his love for basketball, but the way he allowed himself to be part of something he enjoyed, without needing to be perfect. And for a fleeting moment, I remember what it felt like to simply sit in the bleachers and smile. Like his motorcycle rides, those evenings on the court were another kind of journey- quiet, a little bumpy, but full of heart.

I absolutely loved high school. I found new friends who introduced me to sports. They had me trying to play volleyball, but I was not good at all, so that didn't last long. Prior to that time, I focused only on academics, which I excelled at, and threw myself into extracurricular activities, like the public speaking club. My first time speaking in front of an audience was nerve wracking! My words came out like a sprinter would run to the finish line. No one, not even me, could understand what I was saying. My English teacher took it upon herself to teach me the tricks of public speaking; when to pause, when to emphasize and when to look at the audience.

I loved learning and delivering the best speeches of some of the greatest speakers of our time, including JFK Jr and Martin Luther King Jr. And who doesn't like Mark Anthony's speech in the play Julius Ceasar? "Friends, Romans, countrymen, lend me your ears" was the line that made me appreciate public speaking.

I also joined the student body, a school-sanctioned "political" group responsible for planning events and activities, like the school intramural events.

I successfully ran as the school treasurer once.

I loved being a part of a team; we planned and executed events, and it felt good to see plans come into fruition, like I accomplished something. For a time, I felt like I was truly thriving, enjoying the best years of my young life.

While high school was a time of personal growth and new experiences, the world outside our campus was changing in ways I hadn't fully grasped- until one day, the news shattered our sense of normalcy.

News arrived that cast a shadow over everything. One of our teachers made the announcement in class; Benigno "Ninoy" Aquino Jr., the staunchest political opponent of President Marcos, was assassinated. He was shot on the tarmac while deplaning after returning to the Philippines from a three-year exile. Later, I saw the news coverage on tv. It showed his body sprawled, bloody on the tarmac. It was a gruesome scene, one that I have never seen before. It sent a shockwave through my body. My view of the world has been altered, from almost predictable existence to uncertainty. I also realized then that the world I knew was about to change. It ignited in me a curiosity of what was to come, but it also was tinged with fear. Fear of the unknown, perhaps. Or maybe just fear of change.

It was a deep curiosity mixed with a fear of what was coming. As I witnessed my teachers and parents whispering in hushed tones, I began to sense that something bigger than me was unfolding. In the days and months that followed, my curiosity would transform into a hunger for knowledge. The more I learned about Ninoy Aquino- his courage, his sacrifice- the more I understood that politics wasn't just something to be feared. It was something we could influence. His death became the catalyst that opened my eyes to the fragility of freedom and the power of collective action.

Up until that moment, politics had felt like background noise- something the adults argued about, something on the news that didn't quite touch me. But Ninoy's death made it real. It made it personal. There he was, a man who dared to speak against a dictator, gunned down the moment he set foot on home soil. It felt like the rules had changed overnight, like the ground beneath us had shifted. Suddenly, being outspoken wasn't just brave- it was dangerous.

I remember how quiet the classroom was after the teacher's announcement. The kind of silence that follows shocking news, when everyone looks around for confirmation that they heard it right. Some of us didn't even know who he was at the time, not really. But we knew this was big. We could feel it.

That evening, my father sat unusually still in front of the television, his jaw clenched. My mother was quiet, her face pale and unreadable. Even the usual clatter in the kitchen had stilled. The image on the screen showed Ninoy's lifeless body slumped on the tarmac, his white shirt soaked in blood. A scene so brutal, so jarring, it seared into my memory like a brand. I couldn't unsee it. I won't forget it.

And with that image, something inside me began to stir. A kind of awareness, heavy and sharp. A question that hadn't been fully formed until that day: What kind of world are we living in? One where people disappear. Where speaking the truth could get you killed. Where even the most powerful voices could be silenced with a single bullet.

That was the moment I started paying attention. To conversations whispered in corners. To the subtle ways people avoided certain topics. To the tension that seemed to hum under the surface of everyday life. I didn't have the words yet, but I was beginning to understand what it meant to live under Martial Law- not just the curfews and the checkpoints, but the fear. The silence. The knowing looks between grown-ups who had learned when to speak, and when to say nothing at all.

High school continued, and so did the world around us. But I wasn't the same girl who first arrived at the boarding house, clutching her brother's hand and burning rice on the stove. I was growing- not just in responsibility, but in awareness. That scar on my wrist might've reminded me to stay present in the kitchen, but Ninoy's death reminded me to stay awake to the world.

It was the beginning of my political awakening. A slow, painful peeling back of the layers of comfort and naiveté. And just like the steam that burned me when I wasn't paying attention, this moment scorched something inside me. It left a different kind of scar- less visible, but no less permanent.

Looking back now, I can see how those formative years- the moments of change and challenge- shaped my worldview and deepened my awareness. The daily rituals of my youth- sweeping the floors with a walis, braving the crowded jeepneys, and sharing rides on my father's motorcycle- seemed mundane at the time. But now, I see how these moments were full of quiet lessons. Just as the walis swept away dust, my experiences helped me sweep away the ignorance I once had about my world.

Even a passing comment from Sister Maria stayed with me. When I asked her a simple question about where she was going, she gently told me that in her culture, that kind of question might be considered too personal. She wasn't unkind, just honest- and something about that small exchange made me pause. It was the first time I truly understood that the world was much bigger than my little town, that people carried different customs, different expectations, and that respect sometimes meant holding back curiosity. That realization left a quiet mark on me; one I didn't have the words for then-, but I carried it with me.

Like the unpredictable rides on a jeepney, my young life had already been a journey of bumps, unexpected turns, and moments that shaped me. Along the way, I picked up lessons- some loud, some quiet, but all unexpected. Little did I know then that becoming who I was meant to be would one day require me to tap into those lessons... whether I was ready or not.

Chapter 9: Shadows and Sunrises

"History is made not only in the halls of power but in the quiet awakenings of ordinary people."

-The Author

I was too young to understand the weight of the word "dictatorship", but I knew its presence. I felt it in the whispered conversations of adults, the stiffening of my mother's posture whenever the radio mentioned Marcos, the way teachers at school carefully chose their words. My entire childhood and adolescence unfolded under the shadow of Martial Law, a time when fear and uncertainty were the backdrop of our daily lives. While the nation struggled under the weight of dictatorship, my family and I were navigating our own challenges within a society forever altered by one man's grip on power. Growing up under this oppressive regime, I often felt the heavy silence or the involuntary resignation to the current political climate- a quiet tension that made us all wonder what the future held.

Even as a child, I sensed that the world outside our small home was not as it should be. I never understood why we had to be inside at a certain time every night. "We have to hurry home," my mother would urge if we were out after sunset, "it's almost curfew!" At the time, I didn't question it- I only knew that my mother's voice carried urgency, and that breaking this invisible boundary was not an option. Years later, hearing the word "curfew" would bring those memories rushing back.

News traveled in whispers. My father would scan the headlines of the state-controlled newspapers but never commented on what he read. My mother turned the volume down whenever political discussions came on the radio, as if keeping our house quiet could keep us safe. At school, we were taught to respect the "Bagong Lipunan" (New Society) that Marcos claimed to be building. But I could sense the unease in my teachers' eyes when we recited patriotic songs. Even as a child, I understood that some truths could not be spoken out loud. And in that silence, I learned to listen differently- to tones, to glances, to what wasn't said.

Ferdinand Marcos Sr, a former soldier who claimed to be the most decorated war hero in Philippine history, built his political career on a foundation of exaggeration and fraud. Documents have since revealed that his supposed military accolades were grossly inflated, if not entirely fabricated. After serving in the House of Representatives and the Senate, Marcos successfully ran for the presidency in 1965. His first term coincided with a period of economic growth, earning him widespread popularity. Riding this wave of approval, he easily secured re-election. But as his second term progressed, cracks in his leadership began to show. In 1972, before his second term ended, Marcos declared Martial Law, using the threat of communist insurgency as his pretext. This move allowed him to rewrite the constitution and consolidate absolute power.

Under Martial Law, Marcos weaponized the military, silenced the media, and unleashed violence against his political opponents, Muslims, suspected communists, and even ordinary citizens. From 1972 to 1986, his administration issued 2,036 Presidential Decrees- an astonishing average of 145 per year. To put this in perspective, only 37 laws were passed in the Philippines between 2013 and 2015. Many of Marcos' decrees are still in effect, a testament to the enduring impact of his regime.

By 1981, as opposition to his dictatorship grew, Marcos attempted to placate the nation by holding a national election- one he predictably won. But his popularity took a nosedive in 1983 following the assassination of his most prominent political rival, Senator Benigno "Ninoy" Aquino Jr., as he deplaned in Manila after a three-year exile. The public outrage was palpable, fueled further by an economic collapse and leaked documents exposing Marcos' fraudulent war records and financial corruption. As his grip on power began to weaken, Marcos called for a snap election in 1986, aiming to legitimize his rule.

Want to guess the outcome? Unsurprisingly, he declared himself the winner. However, allegations of widespread electoral fraud, coupled with increasing political unrest and human rights abuses, became the catalyst for the People Power Revolution of 1986- a historic uprising that would finally end his reign.

I didn't understand everything that was happening in February 1986- I was only fifteen- but I could feel the air. Neighbors gathered around small radios, faces tense. My father, usually reserved, clenched his fists when reports of massive crowds in Manila came in. "This is it," he muttered under his breath.

The People Power Revolution was a peaceful yet powerful campaign of civil resistance against electoral fraud and the violence of the Marcos regime. From February 22 to 25, 1986, tens of thousands of civilians-students, priests, nuns, political opponents, and ordinary citizens-bravely formed human barricades between military tanks and the masses in Manila. Anti-Marcos soldiers joined the protesters, creating a tense standoff that teetered on the brink of violence.

To prevent a bloody confrontation, U.S. President Ronald Reagan—long an ally of Marcos—sent a message through Senator Paul Laxalt, advising the dictator to "cut and cut cleanly." This was not merely a suggestion; it was a turning point. With mounting pressure from both domestic uprisings and international allies, Marcos fled the Philippines with his family aboard U.S. military helicopters and was granted asylum in Hawaii.

It was an irony: the same superpower that had once backed his regime now ushered him out.

In his place, Corazon "Cory" Aquino—the widow of his slain political rival Senator Benigno "Ninoy" Aquino Jr.—assumed the presidency. Her rise was more than symbolic; it marked a new chapter in Philippine democracy. Finally, after years of oppression, the people of the Philippines forced a dictator out of office, not with weapons, but with unity and courage. And yet, the shadow of U.S. involvement—both in propping Marcos up and in facilitating his exit—stayed a reminder that our fate had never been entirely our own.

When news broke that Marcos had fled, I saw my mother exhaling- a slow, deep breath, as if releasing years of held tension. The fear that had lingered in our home for so long was beginning to lift, like a heavy mist burned away by the morning sun.

A few days after Marcos fled and the revolution was declared a success, a song called Magkaisa ("Unite") played over radios across the country. Written by Tito Sotto and performed by Virna Lisa, it captured the collective ache and fragile hope of a nation trying to come back to itself.

"Magkaisa... kahit 'di tayo magka-anyo sa iisang layunin, sabay tayong magkaisa."
(Let us unite... even if we do not look alike, in one shared purpose, let us unite.)

The song flowed through streets still resonating with chants and prayers, becoming a kind of balm for the wounds that Martial Law had left behind. It became the anthem of the People Power Revolution- a melody of hope, courage, and unity. At school, the song echoed through the halls. We were taught the lyrics and sang it after the national anthem. One morning, the school choir performed it for the entire student body. Their voices rose like a wave, clear and strong. As I stood among my classmates, I felt something shift within me again. The revolution wasn't just something I had heard on the radio or seen on TV. It was alive in our voices, our drawings, our conversations. I realized that history wasn't just made by the people in the capital or the adults in charge- it was also unfolding in classrooms, in our homes, in our hearts. I was just a teenager, but for the first time, I saw myself as a citizen- with a voice, with convictions, and with the responsibility to pay attention.

To honor the historic event, our school organized an art competition. The theme was the peaceful revolution and what it meant to us. I was eager to join. I had a clear vision in my mind- two hands breaking a heavy chain, with the sun rising behind them. Even though I wasn't much of an artist, I knew someone who was: my brother Jun. So, I went to him and asked, "Want to enter as a team?" He didn't hesitate. "Let's do it," he said, smiling.

We got to work. I described the image I had in my head- the symbolism of broken chains standing for freedom, and the rising sun for new beginnings. Jun listened intently, asked a few questions, then began to sketch. I watched in awe as the scene took shape on the page, as if he were drawing straight from my imagination. The hands were strong but not angry; the sun warm but not blinding. We wanted it to show both struggle and hope.

When we submitted our piece, we weren't sure what would come of it. But to our surprise, we placed- we took third! We were elated, proud, but also subdued. We understood what it had taken for the country to reach this moment. And for me, that drawing became more than just a school project- it marked a shift. Until then, politics had always felt distant, something for adults to worry about. But now, I was beginning to see how it touched everything- our family, our freedoms, our future. Creating that artwork with Jun helped me understand that even young people could have a voice, and that expressing what we believed- even with a pencil and paper- was its own quiet form of protest.

I never imagined that the things I witnessed as a child under Martial Law- the silencing of dissent, the manipulation of truth, the gradual erosion of checks and balances- would feel familiar again, decades later and half a world away. Living now in the United States, I find myself unsettled when I see a growing reliance on executive power, or when institutions are weakened in the name of efficiency or ideology. I am not making comparisons, only observations. But once you have lived through the slow tightening of freedoms, you learn to pay attention.

For decades, the United States had largely turned a blind eye to the atrocities of the Marcos regime, prioritizing its military bases in the Philippines to counter China's growing ambitions in the South China Sea. Geographically, the Philippines is vulnerable to Chinese territorial claims, making it a strategic ally for the U.S. While the presence of U.S. forces provided external security, it also enabled the Marcos regime to thrive unchecked, serving his own personal interests as well as American interests at the expense of the Filipino people.

The actual cost of the dictatorship became clear in the aftermath. Marcos and his cronies had ravaged the nation's natural resources, looted the treasury, and left the economy in ruins. According to the Presidential Commission on Good Government (PCGG), formed after Marcos' ouster, the regime stole an estimated $5 to $10 billion from the Central Bank of the Philippines. Marcos' wife, Imelda, became famous for her extravagant lifestyle, earning her the term "Imeldific," which the Oxford Dictionary now defines as ostentatious extravagance to the point of vulgarity.

But the Marcos family's influence was far from over. Imelda returned to the Philippines with her husband's cryogenically preserved body and successfully ran for Congress. Rumors of vote-buying was rampant. In a bitter twist of irony, their son, Ferdinand Marcos Jr., is now the President of the Philippines- a stark reminder of how history can repeat itself. It is imperative to mention, however, that the sins of the father should not be visited upon the son. Thus, he will be measured by his own actions, not his father's. Then history, once again, will be the final judge.

The dictator may have fled, but the damage he left behind would continue to shape the choices of millions, including my own family.

For many Filipinos, survival meant finding opportunities beyond our borders. The Marcos regime may have collapsed, but its economic devastation lingered, forcing countless families to make impossible choices- including members of my own family.

Have you ever wondered why you meet so many Filipinos no matter where you go? Ireland, the UK, Dubai, Australia, the United States, Italy, Singapore- Filipinos are everywhere. Most are highly educated-nurses, radiologists, engineers, medical researchers- but many work menial jobs, such as janitors, housekeepers, or factory workers. These are the Overseas Filipino Workers (OFWs), citizens who leave their families and homes to work abroad temporarily, often under harsh and exploitative conditions.

OFWs endure physical abuse, sexual harassment, and substandard living arrangements, yet they persist because they are the backbone of the Philippine economy. In 2022 alone, OFWs sent home $36.14 billion in remittances, fueling consumer spending and economic growth. They are the Philippines' greatest export, accounting for 75% of remittances, according to the Harvard International Review.

But this success comes at a cost- both for the country and the Overseas Filipino Workers themselves. The Philippines is experiencing a "brain drain" as highly skilled professionals-physicians, engineers, seamen, and more- migrate abroad. According to Dr. Babita Srivastava of William Patterson University, this emigration can undermine a country's intellectual standard, as its brightest minds leave. Educated individuals are the cornerstone of a progressive society; if the best doctors leave, new generations may struggle to receive top-quality education and training, ultimately affecting the quality of patient care.

In my own family, the sacrifices of leaving home for work were not uncommon. I remember how some of my aunts and uncles became OFWs, seeking better opportunities far from the familiar comfort of our province. I personally benefitted from one of my uncles' stints as an OFW.

My Uncle Nardz is the 8th child in my mother's large family, the 5th youngest. By the time they were orphaned, he was old enough to decide for himself whether he would live with us or not. He chose not to. He instead put himself through trade school as a mechanic. With the skills he learned, he applied and was accepted as an OFW in Saudi Arabia. His initial contract was for two years, which he renewed more than once.

But for me, the impact of migration wasn't just financial- it was also intellectual. Whenever my uncle came home from working abroad, I didn't care about the chocolates or souvenirs he brought- I wanted his books. While my siblings and cousins excitedly unwrapped their pasalubong (gifts in English), I was already rummaging through his suitcase, my fingers trailing over the spines of paperbacks with creased covers and yellowed pages.

"What new books did you bring, Uncle Nardz?" I would ask, practically vibrating with excitement.

Uncle Nardz would chuckle, pulling out a thick novel, its edges softened from being read repeatedly. "This one will make you think," he said, handing me a Robert Ludlum book, "The Bourne Identity".

And he was right. Jason Bourne's world of espionage, double identities, and high-stakes deception thrilled me, but it also did something else- it planted seeds of curiosity in my young mind. The twists, the betrayals, the hidden truths within the pages made me wonder: What secrets existed in real life? Were the stories we were told about our country- the government, the history, the war heroes- just as carefully crafted as the plotlines in my uncle's books?

I devoured every novel he gave me, including the other Bourne sequels, escaping into worlds far removed from my own while unknowingly sharpening my ability to question, to think beyond what was presented as truth. My uncle probably didn't realize it at the time, but in handing me those books, he wasn't just giving me stories- he was giving me a new way of seeing the world.

I never asked him what it felt like to leave everything behind for a job in a foreign land, or how he coped with the long stretches away from home. I was too young to understand the weight of that kind of choice. But even then, I sensed that there was more behind his easy smile- something quiet, maybe even lonely, tucked behind the creases of his smile.

When I see him again, I'll make sure he knows just how much I appreciated him- not just for the books, but for being a part of the foundation that shaped who I am today.

There was also a time when my mother almost left. She had an offer- housekeeping in Hong Kong, good pay, a contract for two years. We didn't talk about it much, but I overheard her late-night conversations with my father. "I can't," she said one evening, her voice thick with emotion. "Who will raise them?"

The decision was made. She chose to stay, sacrificing financial opportunity for something she believed was more important: being present. Later, she explained to me and my younger brother, Jun, why she had turned down the offer. She pointed to the families around us- those with one parent abroad for years at a time. They had more money, but their homes were often fractured- discipline issues, teenage rebellion, a sense of distance that no number of remittances could fill.

My mother always believed that the best way to teach was by example. She didn't just tell us why she stayed- she showed us. My mother, always the teacher.

Looking back, I wonder how different my life would have been had she left.

While the remittances from OFWs bolster the economy, they come at a steep personal cost. OFWs sacrifice their happiness, relationships, and sometimes even their lives, leaving behind families and dreams in pursuit of financial stability. This story of sacrifice is born from the economic devastation left in the wake of the Marcos regime- a story of resilience and hardship that began in the 1970s and continues to shape the lives of millions of Filipinos today.

Despite this, the gap between the haves and have-nots in the Philippines remains as vast as the Pacific Ocean. The country is still struggling to recover the stability it lost under the Marcos dictatorship. For many Filipinos, the only way to improve their circumstances is to leave behind everything they know and love, hoping to build a better future for their families. This is the lasting legacy of the Marcos years.

In my travels around the world many years later, I met Filipinos in every country I have visited. They worked in diverse industries, entertainment, housekeeping, healthcare, law, engineering, entrepreneurship, even politics. I once met a woman whose family had been exiled during Martial Law. Her father was an activist, voicing dissent over the corruption and brutality of the regime. Fearing for his life and his family's, they fled. He passed away, having never returned to the Philippines.

"Have you been back since?" I asked her.

"No, and I don't think I ever will. The memories are too painful." She said quietly. The sadness in her voice was so palpable, even all these decades later.

The legacy of the Marcos years is not just etched in history books, but in the hearts of every Filipino who grew up under its shadow. It's their story of pain and perseverance, oppression and endurance. Yet it is also a testament to the Filipino spirit- undaunted, unbroken, and always finding ways to thrive, no matter the odds.

For me, it meant learning early on about resilience, sacrifice, and the power of hope. These lessons, forged in the crucible of oppression and endurance, continue to guide me as I navigate the complexities of my own life.

Long after the smoke cleared and the shock wore off, that image of my elementary school friend's sister- charred, lifeless, anonymous- stayed with me. It wasn't just the horror of death that haunted me. It was the way it happened, how casually violence could erupt, how little her life seemed to matter in the machinery of power. The silence, the fear, the normalization of brutality. I had seen this before. I had lived it. And now, half a world away, the shadows of that era have found me again. The lessons of Martial Law- lessons I thought I had safely tucked away in childhood- come rushing back.

And yet, as I think back to that moment when Corazon Aquino stood at the helm of a people's uprising, I can't help but feel the weight of what didn't last. She rose not through traditional politics, but through the will of a people desperate for change, hungry for light after so much darkness. But in the decades since, only one other woman has won the presidency.

Sometimes I wonder if we, as women, are still learning how to stand with each other when the stakes are high. I've seen how we are taught- subtly, constantly- to compete, to compare, to distrust. Maybe that's why even the most qualified women candidates can lose to men with far less to offer. Not just because of the system stacked against them, but because some of us have yet to unlearn the belief that power only fits a certain shape, a certain voice, a certain face.

It is a shadow that lingers; one not cast by tanks or tear gas, but by something quieter and harder to name. And maybe that's where memory becomes a kind of resistance, remembering not just the victories, but the blind spots. Not just what we fought for, but what we've yet to confront.

Some shadows, I've learned, never fully disappear. They stretch across oceans and generations, lingering in quiet moments when we least expect them- like the sound of gunfire in a foreign city, or the sight of a lifeless body on a road that's not supposed to feel like home. To remember is to refuse erasure. To speak of what we've seen, even when it's painful, is to push back against the silence that once smothered us. In remembering her- in her charred state-, and all the others we were never allowed to mourn or just didn't know how, I carry forward the lessons of those years. Not just the sorrow- but also the strength, the vigilance, and the quiet, steady flame of hope that refuses to be extinguished.

Still, I wonder- if the People Power Revolution had also been a feminist uprising, would things have turned out differently? If we had not only unseated a dictator, but also dismantled the culture that devalues women, might we have built something more lasting? More just? We celebrated the power of unity, of people rising together.

But did we forget to ask: what power do we rebuild with, and who has the privilege to hold it?

Did we also miss the chance to ask: which people were heard, and which were sacrificed in silence?

Until we answer that, the work of the revolution remains unfinished.

Chapter 10: Sixteen and Ashamed

"To be a girl is to be told what you are and what you are not, until you forget who you were."

  -Anonymous

The beginning of junior year was electric with excitement! By this time, I had cultivated a close-knit friendship with three of my classmates-all girls. The four of us weren't just friends; we were a force. We also happened to be in the top 1% of our class. At any given time during the school year, one of us would hold the top honor, a title that constantly rotated among us.

Despite the undercurrent of competition, our bond was unshakable. We did almost everything together: school politics, choir, and the debate team.

I found myself as both their cheerleader and their friendly competitor. Sarah, bold and outspoken, was always quick with her wit and even quicker to defend what was right. She was the friendliest and the loudest, with a worldliness that made her seem always a step ahead of us. Ana excelled in almost all of our classes, and she had the best singing voice among us. She probably was also the most levelheaded. We would tease her that "Let me think about it," was her favorite answer to every question. Then there was Grace who had an analytical mind, solving complex math problems with ease.

Ahh Grace- perhaps because she was the youngest, she was also the most reserved- quieter than the rest of us, but brilliant in her own right. She had a sharp mind but sometimes took a little longer to catch on to our jokes or wordplay, which only made us love her more. Whenever she finally got it, her face would light up with realization, and we'd burst into laughter, half at the joke and half at the way it had taken her an extra beat to catch up. "You guys are so mean," she'd protest, swatting at us playfully, but she knew it was all in genuine fun. In truth, we admired her; being younger never stopped her from keeping up with us academically, and her presence made our little group feel complete.

We laughed at the silliest things, whispered about our crushes, and bantered about everything under the sun. Sure, we competed academically, but it was a friendly rivalry that pushed us to be better. Sometimes, we'd even place playful bets on who would ultimately end up as valedictorian. It wasn't just about the competition- it was about dreaming big together. Looking back now, I know those friendships turned high school into one of the best, most vibrant times of my life.

As junior year unfolded, the excitement wasn't limited to academics. My friends and I started to dream out loud about the future. College was no longer some distant concept- it was on the horizon, just within our grasp. We poured over scholarship opportunities and mapped out our plans. I had my sights set on law school, Ana dreamed of becoming a stewardess (or "flight attendant," as we'd call it now), Grace aimed to be a doctor, and Sarah, ever the free spirit, was still undecided. We were giddy with anticipation, bubbling over with the kind of hope only teenagers can feel. The future stretched before us like an open sky, full of endless possibilities.

Midway through the year, I got news that felt like a dream come true. My grades qualified me for a prestigious scholarship sponsored by my father's employer- a large, U.S.-based company operating in the Philippines. But this wasn't just any scholarship; it was the kind that could send me to any college of my choice, not just in my country but in the United States. The scholarship was more than an opportunity; it was a golden ticket to the life I envisioned.

I remember the exact moment I found out. We were home and my dad called me while holding a letter in his hands, his expression unreadable. My stomach churned as I walked towards him, running through every likely reason I could have been summoned. Had I done something wrong? Was there an issue with my grades? But then he smiled- a warm, knowing smile that made my breath catch in my throat.

"You've been chosen," he said simply, handing me an official letter.

I was jumping up and down with joy, gripping the letter so tightly that the edges crumpled beneath my fingers. This was it. This was my chance to escape the small-town expectations that had always felt too tight around me, to prove that I was capable of more. The weight of it all- the pride, the pressure, the sheer magnitude of what lay ahead- settled in my chest like a heavy, thrilling secret.

My father watched my reaction in silence, his face brimming with pride. My mother hovered nearby; hands clasped tightly together. When he finally looked up, his eyes glistened with emotion I rarely saw.

"You did this," he said, his voice thick. "You earned this."

The pride in his words was everything. But beneath it, I sensed something else- worry. My parents had always encouraged me to dream big, but I knew the idea of my leaving, crossing oceans to chase an education, terrified them. And if I was honest, it terrified me too. If I went through with applying and actually got accepted, I would be a fish out of water. I have never been out of the country before! How often can I come home? And then there's money. Even though my tuition and board are going to be paid for, how about incidentals? I might have to get a part time job, but what kind of job? I never really had a job before either! But the excitement of getting the scholarship overshadowed any worries. I did it, yes! I wanted to share the great news with my friends but decided to wait until all the paperwork was in place. But before I could share my triumph, another piece of news would arrive - one that changed everything.

I never lacked confidence, but high school was also a time of self-discovery. One day during homeroom, our teacher gave us an exercise: Ask a classmate or two to write down how they perceive you- how they see you as a person. They will hand you back what they wrote, and you reflect on it.

Curious, I picked a couple of classmates. When they handed me their responses, I was taken aback. One of them had written, you come off as aloof.

Aloof? I had never seen myself that way. I didn't realize that my confidence might rub some people the wrong way. It was the first time I truly thought about how my words and actions affected others. I was never mean, but from that moment on, I became more mindful of how I spoke and to whom I was speaking. Still, I couldn't shake a new, unsettling feeling-doubt. For the first time, my confidence wavered. Had I been too unaware of how others saw me?

That's why receiving the scholarship meant more than just an academic achievement- it was validation. It reminded me that maybe I was fine just the way I was. You can't please everyone, I told myself, echoing the wisdom of my teachers and my parents. And for the first time, my dreams didn't feel like distant hopes; they felt real. They felt within reach.

And then there was him. The new boy in town.

He was a local, but he had spent the last few years studying in the big city. When he returned, it was as if he carried some of that city magic with him- an effortless confidence, a certain charm that made heads turn wherever he went. He wasn't just handsome; he was magnetic, the kind of boy who made girls giggle nervously and boys unconsciously straighten their posture in his presence.

I had never really been the type to fall easily. Sure, I'd had crushes before- fleeting, innocent feelings that never seemed to last beyond a few shy smiles and daydreams. But this was different. He was different. And somehow, against all odds, he noticed me.

It started with stolen glances across the school courtyard, the way his eyes lingered a second longer than they should have. I told myself it was nothing. Wishful thinking. But then came the first real conversation.

It was after school, and I was gathering my books when he strolled over, casual but deliberate.

"You always walk so fast," he remarked, smirking. "What, afraid someone's going to beat you to the library?"

I laughed, surprised by his teasing. "Some of us actually enjoy studying," I shot back.

His grin widened. "So that's your secret."

From that moment, he had a way of making me feel seen- as if there was something special about me that only he could recognize. He paid attention in ways that felt intoxicating. The way he leaned in just a little closer when we talked, like every word I said mattered. The way he remembered the smallest details, my favorite color, the book I was reading, the fact that I hated waking up early but somehow still managed to be the first one in class.

He made me laugh, too. Really laugh. Once, during a school event, he whispered a joke in my ear so unexpectedly funny that I snorted, completely unfiltered. I turned red with embarrassment, but he just chuckled and said, "That's the best sound I've heard all day."

It was moments like that- the playful teasing, the late-afternoon walks, the way he made me feel like the most interesting girl in the room- that drew me in. One by one, my defenses crumbled.

My friends noticed before I even admitted it to myself. "You like him," Ana teased one afternoon, nudging me with her elbow as we sat in our usual spot under the acacia tree.

"I do not," I protested, but my warm cheeks betrayed me.

Sarah just raised an eyebrow. "Sure. And I don't like winning debates."

The truth was, I was already falling.

When he finally asked me out, it felt inevitable- like something that had been building from the very first glance. My heart raced, but I played it cool. "I suppose I could fit you into my busy schedule," I teased.

He grinned. "Lucky me."

And just like that, I was his.

At first, it was exhilarating. The stolen moments between classes, the way his hand fit so naturally in mine, the way he'd squeeze it lightly as if to remind me I'm here, I choose you. We walked to and from school together, sometimes in comfortable silence, other times lost in deep conversations about the future- his dreams, my ambitions.

I convinced myself it was love. How could it not be? He made my heart race. He made me feel beautiful. He made me believe. He also made me feel like the belle of the ball. I knew other girls also found him cute, so I was on cloud nine, the "it" girl.

I didn't notice the subtle shifts at first. The way my world began to shrink, centering entirely around him. How I spent less time with my friends and more time making sure I was available whenever he wanted to see me. Sometimes it felt like he preferred to be with his friends, but I didn't want to be the possessive girlfriend. So, I didn't let it bother me too much. It didn't feel like a sacrifice- just something that made sense. After all, wasn't love about making not only each other a priority, but also letting the other have space?

But every so often, a tiny voice in the back of my mind wondered- was I making space for him, or slowly making myself smaller?

When my parents cautioned me not to get distracted, I waved off their concerns. "I'm still at the top of my class," I reminded them. "I have everything under control."

My father, always pragmatic, simply said, "Just remember, not everyone who claims to love you will be willing to walk the hard road with you."

I brushed it off. He didn't understand. This was different, I reasoned. I was so consumed by the ecstasy of young love that all I could see, feel and smell were roses. I should have seen it then- the warning signs, the way he subtly shifted the balance of power between us. But I was too lost in him to notice. By the time I did, it was too late.

Whenever we would walk to and from school together, I noticed the side glances from our schoolmates and townspeople; some curious, some approving, others indifferent. One day, as I was walking alone, I passed a neighbor I liked and respected. He motioned for me to stop.

After exchanging pleasantries, he teased, "I see you have a boyfriend!" I laughed and nodded.

"I can see that you like him a lot," he said. "You are a smart girl. You can go places. But be careful- love can make you stupid."

I thanked him for his concern and walked away, thinking that would never be me.

I realized much later how wrong I was.

As the school year wound down and we geared up for summer break, my friends and I made vague plans to meet up halfway through the summer to talk more about our college goals. But life had other plans. My days began to revolve around him. I spent less time with my friends and more time lost in the fantasy of young romance. Even still, I felt a disconnect between us. There were times he was present and with me, but not really.

And then, the unthinkable happened- I was pregnant.

At first, I couldn't believe it. I was in shock. How could I have let this happen? The first signs were easy to brush off- fatigue, a slight queasiness in the mornings. I chalked it up to stress, the exhaustion of balancing school, friendships, and my all-consuming first love. But then, my period was late. Not just a few days- weeks. At first, I convinced myself it was nothing. It had to be. I was too busy to worry, too careful, for this to be real.

Then came the morning when I could no longer ignore the truth. I had woken up nauseous again, my body betraying me. I told myself it was something I ate, but deep down, I knew. Panic clawed at my chest as I mentally retraced every step, every decision that had led me here.

Finally, unable to bear the uncertainty any longer, I found myself staring at a pregnancy test, my hands trembling as I waited for the result. Seconds stretched into eternity, my heart pounding so loudly I was sure it would burst. And then- it appeared. A positive.

My stomach dropped. My breath caught in my throat. No. No, no, no.

This wasn't supposed to happen.

I gripped the edge of the sink, my knuckles turning white. My legs threatened to give out beneath me. The room felt smaller, the walls closing in. The air felt thinner- pressing against my chest. The concrete floor felt cold under my feet, grounding me in a reality I wasn't ready to accept. Suddenly I was freezing, even though I was sweating with anxiousness. As the buzzing fluorescent light above me pierced into my consciousness, my mind raced with frantic questions- How could this be real? What would my parents say? What about school? What about my future?

I wanted to scream. I wanted to rewind time. But all I could do was stand there, staring at that tiny strip of plastic, my entire life rewritten in a single moment.

How could I have been so reckless? I was supposed to be the smart one- the responsible one. The disbelief quickly turned into fear, a bone-deep terror of what was to come. How could I tell my parents? How could I face them, knowing I'd shatter their dreams for me? I had always been the golden child, and being the first born, I was the one they placed their hopes. After all their sacrifices, making sure my siblings and I went to good schools even though we could hardly afford it, and getting us clothed and fed even if they had to take the food off their own plates. Now, I would be the one to break their hearts.

How would I care for my baby?

Then there was the shame. Shame for my parents and shame for myself.

My parents always warned me about being careful when dating, especially when they realized how much I fancied the new kid in town. "You don't want to lose your head," my mother said. "You have the whole world in front of you. You do not want to limit your options." I would nod but not say anything. Looking back now, I think they trusted me to make the right choices. I was the smart one after all. What a mistake that was!

It is amazing how big the shame is of being pregnant out of wedlock in a society that prized virtue and respectability more than anything else. The shame of letting myself down, letting my family down, and derailing everything I had worked so hard for. All my lofty dreams, the scholarship, law school, a bright future- evaporated in an instant, replaced by a suffocating sense of failure.

For days, I rehearsed the conversation in my head, crafting words that would make him understand. We can do this. We'll figure it out together. I imagined him pulling me into his arms, telling me he'd stand by me no matter what.

Reality was crueler than my daydreams.

When I finally gathered the courage to tell him, I could see it in his eyes before he even spoke- the flicker of panic, the way his body stiffened, how his gaze darted away.

"You're sure?" he asked, his voice barely above a whisper.

I nodded; my throat was too tight to speak.

Seconds stretched between us, heavy and unbearable. Then, he exhaled sharply and ran a hand through his hair.

"This… this isn't what I want," he said, the words slicing through me like a blade.

I stared at him, waiting for him to take it back, to say something- anything- that would make this less painful. But he didn't.

"But we love each other," I whispered, my voice shaking. "We can make this work."

He shook his head. "I can't do this. I have plans. This isn't part of them."

The finality in his voice was like a slap. My breath hitched as I fought back tears. What about my plans? I wanted to scream. What about everything we said?

And then, as if breaking my heart wasn't enough, he twisted the knife.

"You know, some of your own family members aren't even your biggest fans," he said, his voice low, calculated. "They think you're too proud, too confident for your own good."

I blinked, momentarily stunned. Was he really saying this now? Trying to make me doubt myself when I was already at my lowest?

But even through the fog of hurt, I saw it for what it was- a desperate attempt to deflect blame, to make me question myself instead of him. I refused to let him have that power. Suddenly, the perfectly charming boy I fell in love with was replaced by the cold, indifferent person standing in front of me. What happened to that warm inviting smile that drew me in? Was he always this indifferent? Callous even? Was I too blindly in love to see? Or was he just as uncertain, even scared like me?

"I don't believe you," I said quietly, my voice steadier than I felt, as I shook my head to clear my thoughts.

His expression faltered for a split second before he recovered, shrugging like it didn't matter. But I knew it did. I knew he had been hoping to plant a seed of doubt, to make me wonder if I had brought this on myself.

I may have been young, heartbroken, and scared- but I wasn't naive. Not anymore.

And then came the final blow.

"I think… I think we should break up."

My heart stopped.

I felt myself shrinking under the weight of his rejection, the heat of humiliation creeping up my skin. I wanted to run, to disappear, to rewind to a time when I still believed he loved me. But it was too late.

Days later, I heard the whispers- he had moved on. With her. One of the prettiest girls in our class.

The shame was suffocating. I had not only lost him, but I had lost myself

I had been sidelined. Rejected. Abandoned.

The shame deepened. The embarrassment consumed me. Every glance felt like a judgment. Every whisper felt like a condemnation.

I was sixteen years old- pregnant, heartbroken, and lost. My future, once so bright and promising, now seemed impossible to grasp. I didn't know how to tell anyone, not even my parents; I was too ashamed. I felt alone, isolated, on an island of my own creation.

I considered my choices. What were my choices? I asked myself. What options did I have that did not involve shame and heartache? My mind could not fully grasp the enormity of my situation, let alone find an answer. Then I remembered my mother's loving gaze at my father's face- a face etched with sacrifice- as if she were looking straight at me. It lit, somewhere deep within me, a faint spark of determination that began to flicker. I didn't know what the future held, but I knew one thing for sure: this would not be the end of my story.

"They were never just girls. They were storms in a soft skin."
  -Nikita Gill

Chapter 11: Judgment Day

"Shame is a soul-eating emotion."
  -Carl Jung

It began as whispers- soft enough to ignore, at first. But soon, they grew louder, crueler, reshaping my name into a warning, my story into a scandal. The smart girl, top of her class- pregnant. And worse, abandoned.

I remember standing outside the school courtyard when I caught my name, followed by hushed laughter. My ears burned. The cement under my feet felt like it might give way. The whispers never stopped. "His family doesn't like her anyway. They like the new girl better."

Worse, one of my closest friends, Sarah, was walking arm-in-arm with the new girl, like they've been friends for a long time. That cut deeper than anything the gossip ever said. I felt betrayed, all over again.

We never had the opportunity to hash things out, and I didn't seek one. Months later, we saw each other by chance. We acknowledged each other's presence, but it was very awkward. I could see the unease, perhaps the guilt in her eyes. But I didn't address it. I knew she felt bad, and I wasn't in a place to make her feel better.

For years after that, we didn't speak. We still haven't. I never felt the need to confront her. I didn't actively avoid her either, but I did let the distance grow naturally. I wonder sometimes how she had been all these years. Perhaps one day, we will reconnect and bury the hatchet.

Even as the town fed off my downfall, the weight of judgment didn't just come from strangers. At home, disappointment hung in the air like a storm cloud that refused to pass. I overheard the townsfolk's biting comments: how aloof I was, how they thought I deserved this as a lesson in humility. I suppose I could understand why, but it was still hurtful. My only wish was to disappear- to lock myself in the house and hope the world would move on without me in it. The shame was unbearable.

Upon learning of my pregnancy, the mother of my estranged boyfriend paid me and my family a visit. She offered to have the Ifugao traditional engagement rite, where the two families and the community celebrate the impending marriage. She knew her son and I are no longer together, but it was her family's way of preserving my social standing. It was also as a recognition and acceptance of the fatherhood of the baby.

I appreciated the gesture, but this was nothing more than to salvage public reputation for both families. And it did nothing to assuage the pain so personal, that I dared not share with them.

Both families and our friends gathered on the yard of our house on the hill. The scent of the butchered pig, garlic and vinegar wafted about as the illusion of unity dominated the scene, held together by tradition and pretense. This was supposed to be a joyous occasion; the irony was not lost on anyone. The conversations felt forced, except perhaps when my closest friend, Ana, asked how I was. I smiled and said I was fine. But she knew I wasn't. "This is just for show." I thought bitterly.

The parents of my ex-boyfriend were disappointed with the situation. Just like my parents, they had big dreams and high hopes for their son. Yet here we all were, and we had to figure out a way forward for everyone involved. They were polite but distant- which is in hindsight, I couldn't blame them for.

At home, I couldn't escape the pained expression, the weight of my father's silent disappointment. My mother told me that when my father learned of my unplanned pregnancy, he left the house that night. Not wanting her to see him scream, he walked the dark, winding road, past our neighbors' sleeping homes, the only sound his footsteps and the occasional rustle of banana leaves. The road was deserted, offering him a place to vent. Grief needs its own geography, I suppose.

While my father's heartbreak was a silent storm, my mother's suffering arrived in flames. My mother, my rock, was hurting too. She had already endured so much.

To help supplement our family income, she'd started selling street food at the farmer's market. But a year ago, in a freak accident, her shirt caught fire from the gas stove. I can't even remember where I was when I heard the news. I rushed to the hospital to see her covered in gauze. She'd suffered fourth degree burn on her upper body up to her neck, just below her jaw. I could see the pain on her face each time her burn wounds had to be cleaned and dressed. And that was the only thing the provincial hospital staff could do. Her burn scars were covered by thick keloid that needed to be removed, but the hospital was not equipped to do such procedures.

"I'm okay, anak. Just broken in a different way. But God will mend me in no time." Always leaning on her faith, she once whispered to me, as I held her hand, careful not to touch the gauze.

The Catholic Mission took it upon themselves to find help elsewhere. Luckily, a surgeon in Manila offered to work her case, free of charge. He specialized in skin grafting. My mother's chest, hands and neck required painful skin grafts, which were taken from her thighs.

The Mission helped in the medication. Without their help, my mother's scars would have been ugly. Her chest and neck would have been filled with keloid- pulling her jaw down. She would have been hunched over for the rest of her life. She spent two months in the hospital burn unit undergoing painful skin grafts and recovery.

She was allergic to anesthesia, so she had to endure each procedure without pain management. She would close her eyes and clench her jaw; it broke my heart to see her that way. I had to hold back tears; I had to be strong for her. But the smell of the hospital and the medications nauseated me; I can only last a few hours a day in the hospital.

During that time, my siblings and I were in the care of our Uncle Nardz. He loved music just like the rest of the family, so he used it as a way to distract us from our grim reality. He started teaching us to play guitar and introduced us to one of his favorite bands- Air Supply.

The opening chords of "All Out of Love" floated through the house like a balm. For a few minutes, we weren't burned, abandoned or drowning in debt. We were just kids learning the song. Air Supply became one of my siblings and my favorite bands.

But the responsibility of taking care of my two youngest siblings fell on me. Jun, always self-sufficient, helped where he could.

Hospital bills started to pile up. Even with the financial help from family and friends, my parents still had to borrow from loan institutions as well as individuals. At that time, there was no health insurance, even for government employees. Everything was out of pocket, adding more challenges to an already dire financial situation.

Those two months were a blur for me and my siblings. Each day we went through the motions of my uncle and me cooking breakfast, getting my siblings ready for school and making sure they did their homework when they got home, preparing supper, getting them to bed and doing it over the next day. I don't remember how I felt, I just knew I had responsibilities, and I had to execute.

She was just beginning to recover when this new blow came. I could see the sorrow etched into her face- not just for what had happened, but for what she feared my future would hold.

Between the stares from everyone, the disappointment at home, and the echo of heartbreak, the thought of vanishing- even temporarily- was a lifeline I was willing to grasp.

The easiest way out wasn't an option. But neither was staying home, suffocating under the weight of stares and whispers. Maybe leaving town would give me a moment to breathe, to figure out what was next. Raised in a devout Catholic household, I knew that my mother's faith, and my own, prohibited even the thought of any easy way out. For all my sins, I knew this was something I may not come back from. It felt irredeemable.

And so, I wrestled with the alternative: adoption. My thoughts spiraled in the late hours, looping through impossible choices. Even that wasn't a choice in my mind. If we all are indeed going to face judgment day, I did not want that on my sheet either. But I wanted badly to get away from all the stares, all the judgment. I asked if I could live somewhere faraway from prying eyes until after I gave birth. My parents thought it would be good for me to be away for a few months. Even as my mother accompanied me to a distant city, it took every ounce of strength just to step off the bus. Sure enough, I couldn't last more than a day.

Walking into a strange house was like walking into an abyss- a feeling of foreboding took over me. The couple who was willing to take me in until after I gave birth were kind, friendly even. Dinner was waiting for us when we arrived. They knew my parents, but they were still strangers to me. It was also raining heavily when we arrived, monsoon season, and parts of the first floor were flooding. The floodwater smelled of mildew and waste, a damp rot that clung to the walls and my skin. Maybe it was just the monsoon. Or maybe it was a sign—this place wasn't meant to hold me, not in my most fragile form. We all retreated to the second floor to get away from it.

I felt deeply uncomfortable. The storm swirled around me, and inside me. I wanted to wake my mother up and tell her I didn't feel comfortable here, I wanted to go home. That night as I laid awake and uneasy in bed, I couldn't shake my initial feeling of foreboding. I didn't understand it, but I had a decision to make. And I had to make it fast.

Then, just as suddenly as the rain had started, it stopped. The sun broke through the clouds, and with that my mind cleared. As surely as the sun had risen, my decision was made; I was going home with my mother. I couldn't bear the thought of being away from everyone I knew, my family.

"I want to go home," I told my mother. And she smiled, like she knew all along.

"Let's go home," she said softly, as she put her arm over my shoulder.

So, with my mother's blessing, we boarded a bus and returned home. For the first time since I realized I was pregnant, everything felt certain.

There was a fork in the road, and I took the one I alone would travel.

My mother gave me her unwavering support, knowing full well the burden of judgment that decision would bring. A part of me still clung to a naive hope that perhaps my child's father might take responsibility. Despite the heartbreak he caused me, I was still in love with him. I thought if I pleaded with his family, if I appealed to their sense of duty, they might convince him to marry me.

I turned to my mother for help. She listened patiently, then said the words that would stay with me for a lifetime: "You cannot fix a mistake with another mistake."

Her wisdom was hard to accept, but deep down, I knew she was right. Forcing him to take responsibility wouldn't bring the outcome I hoped. It would only create resentment and unhappiness. As much as it hurt, I had to let go. Looking back, I'm grateful for her courage in steering me away from that path.

Years later, my mother told me of the support that the Knights of

Columbus and other church organizations gave to my parents. They were encouraging in my parents' decision to fully support me through this ordeal. Some townspeople praised how our family have handled the situation with grace and kindness. I was unaware of it, of course, as I was largely consumed by my own predicament. It comforted me to know that while I was wallowing in shame, others had stood by my parents- just as they stood by me.

And then there was school. I was about to start my senior year, but I knew I couldn't attend a Catholic high school while pregnant. Everyone in town already knew about my situation, so it wasn't long before the school staff found out as well. I didn't know how to approach the administration, so I turned to my favorite nun for guidance. Together with my mother, we met with the school principal. She brought the issue to the Parent Teacher Association (PTA), and we all decided together that it would be in my best interest if I took a break from school. I felt a sigh of relief. I certainly didn't want to be a spectacle in school.

There was also the following year to discuss. The PTA suggested I find another school. They argued that I was no longer a suitable role model for other students.

I understood their reasoning, but the thought of leaving broke my heart.

My mother sat quietly and, per usual, waited for a pause in the conversation, stood up, looked everyone in the eyes.

"If you could, please give my daughter a chance to speak." She said, with a smile.

I stood up gingerly, nervous and overwhelmed, the room suddenly feeling cold and closing in on me. I cleared my throat and pleaded for a second chance, to be allowed to return after giving birth.

I received their decision a few days later: I would be allowed to come back and finish my senior year, but on one condition- I would not be allowed to compete in the honor rolls for valedictorian. I was numb. No reaction: I just took it. Like a felon receiving his sentence. It was my judgment and accepted it. At that point, I didn't care. I also accepted that my dream of delivering a valedictory address had been snatched away- just like that, right before my eyes. I had lost so much already. All I wanted was to graduate high school, to salvage what I could of my future. So, I signed the agreement. What other choice did I have?

My scholarship was another matter. It was my lifeline, my one remaining chance at a better future. Losing it would have been devastating. With my parents' help, we approached the sponsors. My father pleaded my case; I was a good student who made a mistake and who needed a second chance.

"One year of deferment, that's all we are asking," my father said.

Thankfully, they agreed to let me defer the scholarship for a year, allowing me to reapply once I graduate. I was grateful for their compassion, but it was bittersweet. The dream of studying abroad- the dream I had nurtured for so long- was gone. The weight of everything, my shattered plans, my lost love, my diminished prospects- was almost too much to bear. For so many nights, I cried myself to sleep. I mourned everything I have lost; my first love, my dream of perhaps delivering my valedictory address and my dream of studying abroad.

But through it all, my mother stood by me. Her strength gave me the courage to face each day, to keep moving forward even when the road ahead seemed impossibly steep.

At the time, it felt like my life had shattered into pieces too jagged to ever fit back together. I was still a teenager, barely able to process what had happened, let alone imagine a path forward. I didn't yet understand that sometimes survival doesn't look like triumph- it looks like staying. Like showing up to finish something you started, even when everything has changed.

I would wake up and go through the motions- take my prenatal vitamins, read the same pages of my old science books, help out at home, brush my hair, try not to cry. And every once in a while, I would catch a glimpse of the girl I used to be in the mirror- the one who dreamed big, who answered every question in class, who believed in a future outside the limits of our small town. She felt like a ghost.

But there were flickers. A moment when my mother stroked my hair while I rested. A neighbor dropping off boiled bananas and fish without saying a word. A classmate who passed by and simply said, "Hang in there."

These tiny mercies stitched something together in me- no longer the old version of myself, not yet the new one. Just a girl in the in-between, gathering strength not from applause, but from endurance. I didn't know then that this, too, was a kind of becoming.

Life doesn't end with heartbreak, nor with judgment. It shifts, it bends, and sometimes, it leads to places we never imagined. And for me, the road ahead- the fork I had chosen- though uncertain, was one I would walk with my head held high. I didn't know where it would lead, but I knew it was mine to walk. And just behind me was my mother- steady, unwavering- bearing my burdens when I could not, guiding me when I was lost, and walking beside me until I was ready to walk alone.

The world outside had already passed its judgment, and I had become fluent in shame-its posture, its silence, its sting. But after a while, the noise around me quieted, not because it ceased, but because something louder began rising inside me: the weight of what was happening within. The stares, the whispers, the cold shoulders- they were no longer the sharpest knives. What pierced the deepest was the dawning realization that my life was no longer just mine. That something-someone- was beginning inside me. And with that, everything would change.

They called it judgment, but it felt more like rebirth. My sentence had been written, but I was writing the footnotes in real time- with breath, with stubborn hope.

"Shame may have tried to eat my soul. But it never got my spirit."

Chapter 12: A Different Kind of Beginning

"Still, like air, I'll rise."
  -Maya Angelou

I felt like my close friends were embarrassed for me. Perhaps they even felt sorry for me. They still visited, but something had changed. I could feel it in the way their laughter came less easily, how conversations seemed forced, as if they were carefully choosing their words around me. We used to talk about the silliest things- our favorite teachers, the latest crushes, our plans for college. Now, everything felt heavier, more serious.

Once, one of them said, "You know, it seemed like you were singing about your future last year at Intramurals."

"What do you mean?"

"When you sang Papa Don't Preach by Madonna for the talent portion of Miss Intramurals. The words feel kind of... prophetic now."

I remember blinking at her, caught off guard. "But the line I'm keeping my baby- that was about my boyfriend," I replied. And at the time, that was the truth.

I think about that conversation sometimes, especially when one of them brings it up with a laugh that carries a trace of something else, wonder, maybe, or disbelief. Was it a premonition? It seems incredulous- but perhaps not. Who knows?

Those were the kinds of conversations we had then. Gone was the innocence of youth. Gone was the wide-eyed anticipation of the future. They were moving on with their lives, and I was stuck in place. Senior year had started without me. While they buried themselves in schoolwork, took part in extracurricular activities, and filled out college applications, I was in a holding pattern. Time had stopped for me, yet it was moving fast for them. I watched from the sidelines, excited for them but afraid for myself. Where do I go from here? How do I move forward? What have I done with my life?

I never asked my siblings how they felt about it all. At the time, Jun was 14, Bugsy was 12, and Chris was only 9- still children themselves. Jun and I went to the same high school, so I knew he was well aware of everything. I'm sure, in passing moments, I wondered how he was processing it all. But I was too consumed by my own storm of emotions- shame, fear, confusion- to truly consider how my pregnancy was rippling through their lives. Looking back now, I can only imagine how it must have affected them. In a small town like ours, gossip spreads faster than wildfire. The whispers in classrooms, the sidelong glances in the hallways; those things have weight, especially on young shoulders. My siblings had to carry the same gossip I did, without the same power to respond or defend.

If they were angry, I never saw it. If they were ashamed, they never let it show. Not once did they lash out or make me feel like I had brought disgrace to the family. Maybe they didn't know how to talk about it. What words do you even use at that age to name something so complicated? Or maybe they were just trying to protect me, sensing I was already cracked open enough. So, we all moved through it in silence, each of us holding a piece of the weight, but never speaking of it aloud.

It wasn't until years later that my sister finally shared her side. She told me that back then, when the news broke, she didn't know how to feel. She was just a sixth grader, newly transferred to the elementary school near my high school. Everything was unfamiliar to her, and suddenly her world was tangled up in a secret that wasn't hers. She remembers worrying about what others would say, not because she was ashamed of me, but because she hated the idea of anyone talking badly about her Ate (pronounce a-te', the Filipino word for respect for an older sister). But then she saw our parents stand by me- no drama, no accusations, just quiet, steady support. So, she followed their lead. That became her anchor. She found comfort in her new group of friends, too, girls wise beyond their years, one of whom simply said, "Ignore the gossip. It's people with nothing else to do."

That kind of loyalty- the kind that doesn't need to be shouted or written in letters, the kind that just is- stayed with me. At a time when I felt like the world was pointing fingers, my siblings never pointed theirs. They held my name gently when others threw it around carelessly. And even in silence, their love was loud.

But love, even when present, doesn't always drown out shame. My siblings' quiet support, my parents' steady presence; it should've been enough. Maybe it was. But back then, I couldn't feel it through the noise in my own head. I had become my harshest critic, echoing the words I imagined others were thinking. I internalized the whispers and let them rot inside me. And as my belly grew, so did the burden I carried. Not just of new life, but of judgment, of guilt, of fear.

My pregnancy was now showing, so I avoided going out in public. The shame was unbearable. Whenever I had to leave the house, I could feel the stares burn into me. I heard the murmurs as I walked past groups of women at the market, their hushed voices just loud enough for me to catch pieces of their judgment.

"Such a waste. She was so smart."

"She thought she was better than everyone else and look at her now."

"Her poor family. What a disgrace."

Every whispered comment was a knife to my heart. I wanted to disappear, to shrink into nothingness. I hated how they looked at me, as if I were something to be pitied, or worse, something to be mocked.

"Will they ever stop judging me?" I wondered. "Will I ever stop judging myself?"

My mother was the only one who could pull me out of my self-imposed exile. She insisted I go on walks.

"For you and the baby," she would say. "You need the fresh air. You need to move."

I resisted at first, but she always offered to walk with me, standing by my side like a shield against the world. She even took me to Sunday mass. She made sure I looked beautiful in my maternity clothes. "You look radiant in your pregnancy. Your clothes should be as beautiful," she told me once. She saw my pain. She felt my discomfort and frustration. And despite everything, she never wavered in her support. She was my rock, even though I had disappointed her. Without her, I don't know how I would have survived.

Then there was the matter of money. How were we going to pay for the hospital bills, baby food, and diapers?

"We will manage somehow," my mother said, as if she could will it into existence. That was who she was- she always found a way. She had an unshakable trust in the grace of the Lord.

But I knew she worried. I could see it in the way she would sit in silence sometimes, staring into space, deep in thought. She never voiced her fears to me, though. She carried the burden quietly, so I wouldn't feel worse than I already did.

And I did feel worse. The guilt was suffocating. I had put her through so much, yet she stood by me without hesitation.

"People's opinions don't pay the bills," she would remind me whenever I was overwhelmed by the weight of judgment.

I clung to those words.

As my pregnancy progressed, the whispers never ceased, but I had bigger things to worry about. My body was changing, my baby growing, and soon, my concerns turned inward- to the life inside me, and the reality of his arrival.

By this time, we knew I had a breech pregnancy. I stayed hopeful that my baby would turn on his own, but as the months passed, he stayed in the same position. The doctors told me in no uncertain words that my baby will not turn, but I still refused to accept it. When I went into labor, I still clung to the hope of a normal delivery. I endured hours of labor, waiting for something to change, but my baby wouldn't budge. His head was lodged between my ribcage, refusing to turn. The pain was unbearable. Time stretched into eternity.

After 24 hours of labor, the doctors made the decision for me; I needed an emergency C-section.

At that time, full anesthesia was the only choice, so I had no memory of anything from the time I was wheeled to the operating room until I was in the recovery room. Everything seemed foggy and I was still in pain, but I longed to meet my child. Slowly, I was nursed back to consciousness, and the moment I heard my baby cry, everything else faded away. The exhaustion, the fear, the pain- it was all swallowed by the overwhelming love I felt as they placed him in my arms. I traced my fingers over his tiny face, memorizing every perfect feature. My son. My beautiful, healthy baby boy. My heart was full, yet beneath the love, there was an undercurrent of fear. I had no idea what the future held. I only knew that the road ahead would not be easy.

My parents were in the room when I awoke. My mother, now a Lola-grandmother in our language, held my son as my father, now a Lolo-our word for grandfather- gazed at his face, and for the first time in many months, I saw a genuine smile on my father's face. A happy smile, one that reached his eyes. And his eyes twinkled, almost with pride.

"He is handsome, just like his lolo," he said jokingly, referring to himself.

My mother and I giggled. The sound of our laughter, light and unburdened for once, felt strange in the sterile quiet of the hospital room. My C-section incision ached with every movement, but at that moment, I welcomed the pain. It meant I was alive. It meant I had survived.

Once the anesthesia wore off and I was fully awake, the nurses told me that I needed to start walking. "What? Right now?" I asked, confused because less than 24 hours ago, I had been cut up.

Because my son's head was lodged so far up between my ribs and his umbilical cord wrapped around his neck, they had to extend the incision. Typically, it stops inches below the navel, but mine stretched up past it, reaching about two inches above my navel. It was gnarly looking. On top of that, I developed a rash from the adhesives holding the gauze in place. To say I was uncomfortable would be an understatement.

"If you don't start moving now, your recovery will take much longer," said the nurse. With that, I slowly stood up with the nurse's assistance. As soon as I was vertical, I felt like my whole abdomen was going to drop to the floor. Instinctively, I clutched at it, as a wave of dizziness washed over me while the blood rushed downward.

"That's natural after a c-section," she said matter-of-factly. That was reassuring, but it didn't help with the pain. By the second day, I was up and ready to go.

As the days blurred together in the hospital, one moment etched itself into my memory like no other: the smile on my father's face- it was more than just joy. It was relief. It was acceptance. For so long, I had feared that I had let him down beyond repair. I had imagined him carrying my shame on his shoulders, the weight of it pressing down on him in our small, watchful town. But as he looked at my son, I realized something. My father didn't see a mistake. He saw his grandson. A new life. A new beginning.

Maybe, just maybe, I wasn't as lost as I had believed.

Everyone seemed so happy to see my baby. Friends, classmates, even people I barely knew came to the hospital to visit. I wondered then- did they really care, or were they just curious?

And then there was him. His father. I wondered if he would come. If he would care enough to see our son.

He did. But my feeling of indifference surprised me. I thought I would be over the moon with excitement, or at least happy. But I wasn't at all. Still, I was grateful.

But what did his presence mean? Did it change anything? Would he love our child? Would he step up? Or was this just a fleeting moment of obligation?

I didn't know. I didn't have the energy to think about it. We discussed what to name our son, and we agreed on Mark.

His parents bought my son clothes, and things that an infant needs. They tried to show their support, but their son's responsibility was not their burden. There was an unspoken uneasiness about the whole situation, and I was certain they never wanted to be in it, yet here we were. So, we managed to be civil and respectful of each other. Their other children were supportive, but a bit distant. Perhaps they also felt embarrassed, but they never told me how they felt. I suppose being silent was their own way of dealing with it.

Looking back now, I believe my son's father was doing the best he could at the time. We were both so young. I don't think he ever meant to hurt me. Maybe, in his carefree teenage mind, it was all just a game. As young boys often do, he measured his worth by how many girlfriends he could have- sometimes at once. I carry no bitterness for what happened between us. Not anymore.

But even with that understanding, I was still left to carry the day-to-day on my own. And caring for an infant was harder than I had ever imagined. The sleepless nights blurred into one another, exhaustion wrapping itself around me like a second skin. The constant feedings- sometimes it felt like my soul is being sucked out of me. The diaper changes were relentless and unpleasant, a never-ending cycle of mess and motion. I was just a teenager myself, still healing from an emergency C-section, still trying to make sense of the life I now had to lead. Every movement reminded me that I had been cut open and stitched back together- both literally and emotionally.

But I wasn't alone.

My mother, my father, my siblings- they all stepped in to help. My mother rocked my baby to sleep when I couldn't keep my eyes open. My father ran errands, making sure we had what we needed. My siblings fed him, changed him, held him. They surrounded me, not with judgment, but with quiet, steadfast love. I had fallen, yes. I had fallen hard. But they refused to let me stay down.

For all the pain, for all the fear, for all the nights I had spent wondering if I had ruined my life, I had one thing I never expected to find in the middle of my darkest moment— love.

Not just the love of my family, but the love I felt for my son Mark.

It was terrifying, this love. It was bigger than anything I had ever known. It wasn't just about me anymore. Every decision I made, every step I took forward, would be for him. I didn't have all the answers. I didn't know what the future would look like. But I knew one thing with certainty:

The exhaustion was suffocating, the weight of responsibility over-whelming. But love was stronger, steadier. It had carried me through the pain, the judgment, the fear. And somehow, love would carry me the rest of the way.

I had once wondered if I would ever stop judging myself. But holding Mark in my arms, surrounded by the quiet strength of my family, I began to understand. Grace does not always come with grand declarations. Sometimes, it comes in silence, in sleepless nights, in soft footsteps down the hallway. Sometimes, it simply comes... and stays.

Something inside me shifted- setting the stage for the quiet kind of brave I would need to carry forward.

Chapter 13: The Quiet Kind of Brave

"I am not what happened to me, I am what I choose to become."
 -Carl Jung

Going back wasn't just a return to school- it was a return to the scene of my undoing, but with a new kind of strength.

I went back to the same high school to finish my senior year. It felt like walking into the eye of a storm- nothing felt familiar anymore, even though the walls, the classrooms, and the faces were all the same. The campus had once felt like a second home, a place where I thrived, where I laughed with friends and eagerly planned for the future. Now, every hallway, every doorway, every familiar corner felt foreign, like I was an outsider in a life that used to be mine.

Because I took a year off from school, my brother Jun and I were now in the same senior class. The night before school started, Jun and I sat at the kitchen table, eating silently while our mother cleared the table. He hadn't mentioned that we would be in the same grade now, and I didn't dare bring it up. Instead, I watched him out of the corner of my eye- how he chewed slower than usual, how he drummed his finger lightly against the table as if lost in thought.

Finally, he broke the silence. "Are you ready?" His voice was casual. But there was something else underneath it- hesitation, maybe uncertainty.

He gave me a small smirk, but it didn't quite reach his eyes. "Good." And that was it. No judgment, no reassurances. Just one word.

He acknowledged me when we shared a classroom or activity, and we still bantered as siblings and classmates. But like our father, he rarely shared his feelings, so I never knew how he truly felt about me joining his graduating class. I kept a low profile, not wanting to spark any more conversations about me- besides the obvious.

One afternoon after an exhausting day of classes, I found myself alone in the library, staring at my notebook but not really seeing the words. My head ached from the weight of stares and whispers. I didn't even hear Jun walk up until he slid a book across the table toward me.

"You'll need this for the test," he said simply.

I looked at the book- one I haven't thought to borrow yet. "Thanks," I murmured, surprised.

He shrugged and sat across from me, flipping through his own notes. He didn't have to say anything else. In that moment, I knew: He wasn't embarrassed of me. He wasn't pushing me away. In his quiet own way, he was still my brother.

There I was, still carrying the weight of my decisions, of my past. I had become that girl- the one whose name was always followed by a pause. A whisper. A glance. My presence in class was tolerated but not celebrated. I kept my head down, focused on my schoolwork, determined not to give anyone another reason to judge me.

Academically, I still excelled. I pushed myself harder than ever, burying myself in books and assignments as if I could somehow rewrite my story through sheer effort. But it didn't matter. The conditions under which I was allowed to return meant that I could not qualify for any honors. No awards. No recognition. No standing out. But I still needed to keep my grades up for the scholarship, so I kept pushing forward.

It was a silent punishment, a quiet erasure of my past achievements. I had worked so hard for a future that now seemed just out of reach, and no matter how well I performed, there would be no validation. No moment of acknowledgment for all that I had endured just to make it back here.

The most difficult part, however, was the ever-constant reminder of my transgression. Every day, the gossip mill churned, its whispers following me through the hallways like a shadow that would not leave. I had been the "good" girl- the one with the future ahead of her. Now, I have become the cautionary tale. The one everyone knew about, the one who had fallen from grace.

Once, in the middle of a quiet classroom, I heard a giggle from the row behind me. "I heard she still thinks she's going to college," a girl whispered, not even bothering to lower her voice. My ears burned, but I kept my eyes on my notebook, gripping my pen tighter. I wanted to turn around; to tell her she had no idea what I was capable of. But instead, I swallowed the lump in my throat and reminded myself- I was here to finish what I started. No matter what they thought of me.

There was no escaping it. It was in every conversation, every glance, every smile that felt too forced. They did not need to say anything; I could see it in their eyes. The judgment was suffocating.

It had become routine- walking into the classroom, keeping my head down, slipping quietly into my seat as if I could fold myself into the background. I moved like a shadow, careful not to draw attention, convinced that silence was the safest armor I could wear. That's why I was completely caught off guard when Aimee, arguably the smartest in the class and widely expected to be valedictorian, sat down beside me one day, her smile easy, unbothered- like we had always been friends.

"Hey, do you have the notes from last week? I missed a day."

For a moment, I actually looked behind me, sure she must've been talking to someone else. But when I hesitated, she nudged me playfully. "Come on, don't make me beg. I hear you're the best at this stuff."

It wasn't just that she spoke to me- it was how she spoke to me. Like I wasn't invisible. Like I wasn't the girl everyone whispered about. Like I was still me.

That simple conversation opened something inside me. I hadn't realized how heavy it had been to carry the weight of shame, the loneliness, the fear that I no longer belonged. Aimee spoke to me as if nothing about me needed explanation. Her presence beside me wasn't charity- it was choice.

We became friends. Real friends. She was gracious and grounded, never condescending. She knew about the arrangement I had to make with the school, and she didn't treat me any differently for it.

Rumor had it that her parents were among those who spearheaded the campaign to keep me out of the honor roll. Every so often, she'd tease me:

"You know, you'd probably beat me for valedictorian if you weren't disqualified."

And I'd laugh and say, "No hard feelings," and I meant it. I was just grateful. Whether she befriended me out of guilt in the beginning didn't matter. What mattered was that our friendship had become genuine—and still is, to this day.

We messaged each other sporadically, reminiscing about our time in the drama club.

"Do you remember what plays we did?" I asked.

"I don't remember," she replied with a laughing emoji. "I just remember you were a bride in one. And there was another about an entitled kid who got into drugs. Everything's just a jumble of memories."

"I don't even remember those details!" I responded, laughing.

It felt so ordinary- so beautifully ordinary- to share that kind of memory with someone who had seen me through one of the most difficult chapters of my life. Her friendship was more than kindness. It broke through the shell I had carefully built around myself, the one I thought I needed to survive. With her, I could exhale. I could be carefree again- no judgment, no weight. Just me.

And in some quiet, beautiful way, her acceptance gave others permission to shift their gaze too. Slowly, the walls came down. The whispers softened. I was no longer "that girl." I was just another classmate again.

That gesture warmed my heart more than she probably ever knew. It reminded me that people are capable of immense kindness- if only we allow ourselves to see one another beyond the labels, beyond the rumors. In giving me her friendship, Aimee gave me space. Space to come back to myself. To enjoy school again. To believe, maybe for the first time in a long time, that I still belonged.

Looking back now, I think that was the beginning of my quiet return to confidence- not the kind that shouts or needs to prove anything, but the kind that had always lived inside me. I don't know if I was born with it, or if it was the way my parents raised me. Maybe it was both. All I knew was that I wasn't lacking. Even then. I had just been buried under layers of shame, fear, and self-doubt.

Aimee's friendship, and the slow softening of those around me, helped peel those layers back. Little by little, I started showing up differently. Not as the girl defined by her mistake, but as someone resilient, capable, worthy. I raised my hand more in class. I laughed more freely. I allowed myself to feel hopeful about the future again- even if it looked different than I once imagined.

Years later, I reached out to Aimee to ask if I could share through my memoir those memories of our senior year- the laughter, the quiet companionship, the safety of her presence during such a difficult time. I wanted to honor her the way I remember her: kind, brilliant, steady, and funny in the most unexpected ways. When she replied, her words made me pause. She thanked me for seeing her- for remembering her as a blessing, not just a seatmate or classmate, but a true friend. What she didn't know then, and what I tried to tell her, is that she had been one of my safe places. In a year filled with shadows and judgment, she offered light and grace.

Reading her message reminded me that we often carry silent battles- battles others might never see. Aimee had her own struggles with belonging, with feeling seen. And yet, she saw me. She offered laughter and kindness even when she felt invisible. That is the quiet kind of heroism we often overlook.

We often go through life not knowing how much we meant to someone else. But that exchange with Aimee reminded me that even quiet friendships can leave loud echoes in our memory- and in our healing.

Looking back now, I realize that friendship isn't just about shared notes or walking to class together. It's about how someone makes you feel in your most vulnerable season. Aimee made me feel like I mattered. And if telling this story feeds her soul the way she once fed mine, then perhaps we've both come full circle.

I started to believe again. With that quiet kind of brave, I began to rise.

I even agreed to join the school choir when I was tapped by one of the nuns to be a part of it. At first, I was hesitant. Being on stage again meant stepping into the spotlight, and I wasn't sure I was ready for that. I had grown comfortable fading into the background, keeping my head down, avoiding whispers. With my confidence slowly rising again, I rationalized that in a choir, I wouldn't be alone. I would be one voice among many. So, I said yes.

First, because I love singing. Second, because I felt honored to be asked. And third- maybe most of all- because I needed something to hold onto. A reason to stay connected. A lifeline to the parts of myself I didn't want to lose completely. Music became a kind of sanctuary, a place where I could disappear and still be seen.

Still, even in those moments of song, my thoughts drifted to him.

I often thought of my baby. He was my only true solace in the whirlwind of my new reality. He put everything in perspective, drew a clear line from where I was to where I needed to be. The path ahead was daunting, but it had a finish line. A purpose. A name.

Each time I held him, each time he smiled at me with those innocent eyes, it was as though the world paused, and I could breathe again. In that moment, I felt everything that was pure and untainted. But each smile also carried weight. It reminded me of how much was at stake, how many battles lay ahead that I wasn't yet prepared for.

I used to feel at home in school- surrounded by books, friendly chatter, and the steady rhythm of routine. Now, I felt anxious, restless.

How do you stop a roller coaster of emotions like that? The constant push and pull between the joy of holding my baby and the ache of everything I had lost was exhausting. I often found myself caught in between- yearning for peace, for belonging, for forgiveness.

One day, as we were sitting in the kitchen, my mother said something that would stick with me forever. "Acceptance and forgiveness," she said. "You need to accept that you were young, that you made mistakes. You didn't exercise good judgment, but you did the best you could at the time."

She paused, her eyes filled with understanding, before continuing, "Accept where you are. You're in a small town where everybody knows everything. People will talk, and they will judge you. And that's okay. You can't control that. But you can control how you respond to it."

It wasn't the easy answer I wanted. It wasn't a quick fix.

At first, I resisted her words. "But how do I just let it go?" I asked, frustration tightening my chest. "How do I forgive people who don't even care how much they hurt me?"

My mother sighed, stirring the tea in her hands. "First, you have to forgive yourself. Forgiveness isn't for them. It's for you," she said. "You don't do it because they deserve it. You do it because you deserve peace."

I wanted to believe her, but I wasn't sure how. The pain felt too raw, the wounds too fresh. But deep down, I knew she was right. Holding onto resentment wouldn't change anything- it would only keep me trapped. Her words slowly began to chip away at the guilt I carried, the shame that had settled deep within me. I would normally feel so agitated when I would be told by another classmate of a mean comment made by another, but one time I just reacted with a smile, no ill feelings. I realized that I could choose how I wanted to react to everything around me. I could choose to allow the shame to consume me, or I could accept that I had made mistakes and take steps toward healing.

Her words felt like a balm to my wounded soul. Forgiveness had never seemed so possible, so necessary. But she was right. I had to let go of the anger I was holding onto- for the father, for the people who whispered behind my back, and for myself. Without forgiveness, I could never heal.

"Shame has no place where there is acceptance and forgiveness," she added.

As difficult as it was, I slowly started accepting her wisdom. Slowly, I began to forgive, especially myself. It wasn't a one-time thing; it was a continuous process. But with each passing day, the weight lifted, even if just a little.

The day I was accepted to a university eight hours away from home, I was overjoyed but it also felt bittersweet. I had never imagined that my life would lead me in this direction, but now there it was- a chance to build a future, to create something for myself. My mother was supportive, as always. She offered to take care of my child while I went off to college.

I was grateful for her offer, but a part of me couldn't help but feel guilty. How could I leave my baby behind? The distance would be hard. I would miss him terribly. But I knew it was the right thing to do. I knew that I had to take this step for my future, for his future.

When I graduated high school, it wasn't the celebration I had once dreamed of. No fanfare, no grand ceremony. But I didn't need that. I had already experienced the pain, the judgment, the heartbreak- and I was still standing. That, in itself, was a victory.

As I packed my things and prepared to leave, a mixture of excitement and dread settled in my chest. This was what I had fought for; a second chance, an opportunity to carve out a future that was mine. But the closer I got to my departure, the heavier the realization became.

I was about to leave my son behind.

How do you prepare yourself for that kind of separation? How do you say goodbye to the tiny hands that reached for you in the middle of the night, the soft breath against your skin as he drifted off to sleep? How do you step away from the one person whose existence had changed yours forever?

I knew it was temporary. I knew I was doing this for him, for both of us. But the last couple of years had made me doubt myself, my decision-making process. "What if I am making the wrong decision again?" I thought to myself. My mother, sensing my self-doubt and ever the unwavering support, assured me that she would care for him as if he were her own. I trusted her completely, but trust didn't make the ache in my heart any less painful.

The night before I left, I sat by his crib, watching him sleep, committing every tiny detail to memory- the curve of his nose, the rise and fall of his chest, the way his fingers curled slightly, even in rest.

"I love you," I whispered. "I will make you proud."

And as I boarded the bus to my new life, I felt something I hadn't felt in a long time.

Hope.

It wasn't certainty. It wasn't a guarantee of success. But it was enough. For the first time in a long time, I believed that maybe, just maybe, my story wasn't over yet.

It was only beginning to unfold.

I had stumbled, fallen, broken apart. But I had also loved fiercely, fought quietly, and learned to rise again- this time with purpose. I was no longer the girl chasing perfection, or even the girl drowning in shame. I was someone in between, trying. Becoming.

I didn't have all the answers. I still questioned myself. Still wrestled with guilt. But as the bus pulled away, I realized that the greatest act of love wasn't in holding on. It was in becoming someone worth coming back to.

That morning, I didn't just leave home. I carried it with me.

Even as I found new strength, the world outside kept moving- and soon, I would have to move with it, away from my son, and into the unknown of college life.

Chapter 14: Between Pines and Promises

"All children are born innocent. They deserve our presence, even when life demands our absence."

  -Anonymous

It was a bittersweet feeling, finally graduating from high school and getting ready for college. I was excited to move my future forward, yet my excitement was tempered by the responsibility I was leaving behind.

"You know this is the only way," my mother assured me, her voice steady. She had always been the rock, the one who made difficult choices seem unquestionable. And yet, as I looked at my son, sleeping soundly, I wondered- was this truly the only way?

Her reassurance did nothing to assuage the guilt I was feeling for having to leave my son behind.

I waved from the bus window at my son, and he waved back at me with a big smile on his face, not fully understanding what was going on. I smiled, holding back tears. The glass between us felt more than a window- it felt like the first wall rising between our worlds. I wanted to press my palm to the glass, to freeze the moment, to run back. But the engine roared, and the road pulled me forward.

Leaving home for college felt like stepping into a new world- one filled with both promise and uncertainty. My journey took me to Baguio City, a place unlike any I had ever known. Stepping off the bus in Baguio after traveling all night, I inhaled deeply, the fresh morning air filling my lungs. Back home, the scent of damp earth and rice paddies clung to everything. Here, the pine trees carried a fragrance that made me feel as if I had walked into a different life altogether. The scent of pine trees hung in the air like fresh morning dew. The air was crisp and clean, gently caressing my skin, as the fog rolled softly on the mountainsides. It was almost dreamy, except for the hustle and bustle of city life. Even before the sun rose fully on the horizon, the city was already coming to life: street vendors were rolling out their tables and chairs, the jeepneys were busy picking up their fares as they moved in and out of the city streets, like a symphony settling into its sonata.

A mountain town of universities and resorts, Baguio City is home to the Philippine Military Academy, St Louis University, University of Baguio and a few other universities. It is also home to beautiful parks and golf courses including the Club John Hay- formerly Camp John Hay, a US Airforce base- with its famous par 3 hole called Cardiac Hill, its steep hillside serving as the fairway. Baguio was a stark contrast to the hot landscape of my hometown. It was cooler, quieter, with air that smelled of pine trees instead of humid earth. The city was famous for its winding roads, breathtaking views, and temperate climate. A UNESCO Creative City known for its crafts, folk art, woodcarving, silver craft and weaving, it is a center for education, trade and tourism.

Getting there meant navigating steep, narrow roads that clung to the mountainside, where one wrong turn could send a vehicle tumbling into the ravines below. But despite the daunting journey, Baguio was beautiful. They called it the Summer Capital of the Philippines, a retreat for those looking to escape the unbearable heat of the lowlands.

Baguio City boasts of cultural diversity, mainly due to the presence of students from all over the country and even the world: Korea, Greece, India, Australia, China, Turkey. And they brought with them their cuisines. I had my first shawarma there, my first Indian food, and loved them!

At the heart of Baguio stood St. Louis University (SLU), a prestigious Catholic institution founded by Belgian missionaries in 1911. Its sprawling campus, lined with old buildings and towering pine trees, had an air of quiet discipline. The CICM fathers who ran the school emphasized both academic rigor and religious values- something my mother certainly appreciated.

I had chosen Engineering as my major, a practical choice that I hoped would secure me a good job after graduation. Thanks to my scholarship, I wouldn't have to worry about tuition, and there was even a stipend for room and board. It was a blessing, one that made the difficult decision to leave my son behind a little more bearable.

For my first year, I lived in the school dormitory, a strict and structured environment. Everything was shared- bedrooms, bathrooms, kitchen, dining areas, study halls. There was a curfew at 8 PM, a mandatory study period, and little room for personal freedom. The dorm felt more like a convent than a college dorm. Curfews. Shared spaces. Enforced study hours. A world of rules that pressed in, even as the mountains whispered freedom. My roommates and I tried to push the boundaries where we could, lingering in the common area past curfew, whispering about the TA who, despite our best efforts (and my roommate's terrible serenades), never let us stay up past our allotted time.

At times, I felt trapped, but in a way, the rigid routine helped me focus. I developed good study habits, spent hours buried in books, and soon found myself on the Dean's List.

I was ecstatic to be on the dean's list. But I found one of my classes to be challenging because of the professor. Every time he scanned the room for a volunteer, I felt my stomach tighten. There were only three of us women in a class full of men, and he never let us blend into the background. "Miss, would you care to solve this?" It wasn't a question. It was a test. Perhaps he thought he was encouraging us. Perhaps he thought he was being fair. I thought he was a nuisance. But if he wanted me to shrink, he was mistaken. I made sure I was always prepared, my answers quick and precise, so he would never see me falter. I was glad to finish that class and move on

I eventually found new friends. All of them were in my engineering classes. I became really close to a couple of them, Nicole and Mya. We studied together, hung out with each other. I told them about having a child, they were unfazed by it. We used to pull all-nighters before exams. Well, they did, anyway. I mostly slept the night and woke up incredibly early to study. I found that studying at 4am, even in high school, worked better for me than staying up late. They teased me about it, but they were really sweet, and kind and they made school fun again.

Nicole was a smart sweet person, empathetic to everyone. She grew up just down the street from the University, so we often found ourselves in her family home, either doing homework or just getting away from our hectic daily classes. "Would you like anything to drink or eat?" she would often offer. Mya and I took her offer every so often, being mindful not to abuse her kindness and her family's hospitality.

Mya is from a beach town, a few hours down the bottom of the mountain, from the University. She was smart; we were both in the Dean's List. She was also sweet, and very proper. She was the only one I knew that would laugh into her handkerchief, like a proper lady. It amused me! "You are so proper!" I teased her once. "Stop it!" She said, slightly blushing.

I was the outspoken one of the three of us, so we balanced each other out. At first, I called us the Three Musketeers. Over time, a few others in our class joined our group- mostly men. They became our protectors, and challengers, pushing us outside of our comfort zones. It was they who convinced us to form a hiking group.

And yet, I could never fully embrace the life of a carefree student.

I laughed with my friends, studied hard, even hiked- something I had never imagined enjoying. But no matter how full my days were, the nights belonged to guilt. Was it fair that I was here, building a future, while my son's present continued without me? Each time I let myself enjoy a small moment of freedom, an invisible tether pulled me back, reminding me that my life would always be divided.

I even felt guilty going on a hike with my friends during the weekend, knowing that my mother was back in the province taking care of my son. Laughter always felt half-earned, as if joy needed to be rationed in deference to the child I left behind. I knew my life is different from most of the rest of the students. Am I taking life too seriously? Perhaps.

I immersed myself in schoolwork but no matter how busy I was, a part of me was always elsewhere. Every semester break, every holiday, I rushed home to see my son. His smile, his little arms wrapping around me- it was worth every hour of travel, every ache of missing him. My mother, ever selfless, even brought him to visit me in Baguio when time and finances allowed. Those were short visits, just the weekend, while enduring the grueling eight-hour bus ride each way just so we could spend a few days together. Sometimes I wondered if my mother's patience ever wore thin.

Still, the distance weighed on me. No mother should have to watch her child grow up in fragments, in stolen moments between school breaks. But this was the path I had chosen-the only way forward.

The following year, I left the dormitory. I, along with my brother Jun who is in the same school as me, decided to rent a small apartment together. Money was tight. We ate what we could afford- rice, eggs, vegetables, instant noodles, and the rare slivers of meat, more for flavor than substance. Clothes came from thrift stores, and luxuries were unheard of. But there was no room for self-pity. We had no choice but to succeed. There was no safety net waiting for us, no second chances if we failed. A college degree was our only ticket to a better life.

The school itself had its own set of challenges. Political unrest simmered in the background, both in government and within the student body. Protests were common. Students demanded lower tuition, better resources, more access to technology. These strikes would disrupt classes for days, sometimes weeks. Some of my classmates would take part. Once, I might have joined them. Once, I might have marched alongside them, demanding change. But now, I had no energy for activism, every hour wasted on protests felt like a delay in securing my son's future. Every time classes were suspended, frustration gnawed at me. I watched from the sidelines, frustration simmering. The longer it took to finish my degree, the longer it would take to build a stable life for my son. The world burned, but my battlefield was simpler; survival, one semester at a time.

When yet another student strike shut down the university, I had a choice to make. I could stay in Baguio, waiting indefinitely for classes to resume, or I could go home and be with my son until things settled. The decision was easy. No hesitation, more annoyed than anything, I packed my bags, boarded the bus, and headed back to my province, eager to spend time with my child while waiting for school to reopen.

I took the night trip. The bus rolled through the darkened highway, its engine humming like a lullaby. I leaned against the window, exhaustion tugging at my eyelids. Outside, the world blurred into streaks of shadow and headlights. As the motion of the bus lulled me to sleep, I had no way of knowing that this decision- born of weariness and routine- perhaps have saved my life.

Chapter 15: Fault Lines

"You don't really sleep after something like that. You just close your eyes and wait for the earth to move again."

  -Nicole (from the chapter)

It was a hot, sunny July afternoon, and my son and I were in the kitchen, laughing over something simple. I think it was a game of pick-up-sticks. And then, just like that, the earth beneath us shifted. The kitchen floor lurched, like a boat caught in a violent storm. A deep rumble rose from within the earth, growing louder by the second, like a train barreling toward us from a distant track. The walls groaned and shuddered. The metal pots hanging above the stove clanged violently against one another. I grabbed my son instinctively, my heart pounding so loudly that I could barely hear his frightened wail.

The room spun. Dishes crashed to the floor, the sharp shards scattering at our feet. I couldn't even find my bearings as the world twisted and shifted beneath me. It was like standing on a teeter-totter that tilted beyond control. A sharp crack sounded from outside, followed by a heavy thud- something had fallen. My son clung to me, wailing in fear. "Stay close to Mama," I whispered, my voice shaking as much as my body.

Then, as suddenly as it began, the shaking stopped. Silence rushed in, suffocating. We stood there, frozen, in the stillness, the kitchen intact but the world outside holding its breath. The ground had shifted for only 45 seconds, but it felt like a lifetime.

With my son in my arms, I walked across the street where some neighbors were gathered, still trying to process what just happened while checking on each other.

"How could it be so quiet when people are panicking?" I thought. The usual hum of the neighborhood- chatter from passing tricycle drivers, the distant sound of a radio playing from someone's window, the occasional bark of a dog- was gone. Even the birds seemed to have vanished. The air felt thick, as if the world was holding its breath, waiting for something worse to come. I could feel my own heartbeat pounding in my ears, the weight of my son grounding me even as my legs felt unsteady beneath me.

Then my thoughts went to my sister Bugsy and brother Chris. They were in school when the earth shook. Were they okay? I thought. Luckily one of our neighbors was already in contact with the high school. We were told everyone was ok. Bugsy recounted later that her practical arts class was just finished, and they were about to go up the stairs to the second floor when they heard the principal, "Earthquake, earthquake! Go out to the quad!"

They ran out of the building as fast as they could! Some students were caught in the stampede in the narrow doorways, said Bugsy. Once she was out of the building, she said that they kept stumbling as they ran because the ground was still shaking. When they reached the quad in front of the school building, they watched in horror as the students in the 2nd and 3rd floor of the building scramble out of the building. Thankfully the building stayed intact, and no one was seriously hurt. They all huddled in the quad, and after everyone was accounted for, they were sent home.

I was back in the house with my son when my parents and siblings made it home. We were still processing our own fear when the full scale of the disaster began to unfold. Shortly after, we heard on the news that a powerful trembler measuring 7.7 on the Richter scale and the following aftershocks had laid waste to my college town. "Baguio City is a scene of devastation." Said a radio announcer, his voice trembling with emotion.

Baguio City was in ruins and so were neighboring provinces and cities, including Manila, the capital of the Philippines. The 125 km-long ground rupture had caused damage within an area of 20,000 sq kilometers. Baguio City was one of the hardest hit areas. The earthquake caused dozens of collapsed buildings including hotels, factories, university buildings as well as many private homes and establishments. It destroyed electricity, water, and communication lines in the city. The main vehicular route to Baguio, Kennon Road, as well as other access routes were shut down due to landslides. Damage to the airport limited access only to helicopters.

Baguio City was isolated from the rest of the world for the first 48 hours after the quake.

How about my brother, Jun? He had decided to stay in the city during the student strike. My parents were numb with worry, their faces taut, as my mother fell to her knees in prayer, whispering over and over for his safety. The uncertainty was unbearable. Each hour stretched endlessly, filled with anxious silence broken only by the static of the transistor radio delivering grim updates. It was two long, excruciating days before we finally received word- Jun was alive. The moment the news came, relief flooded our home, and we all cried, my mother clutching her rosary as if it had physically kept him safe.

My parents wanted him to come home as soon as the roads were passable, desperate to see him with their own eyes, but Jun was resolute. "I am more useful here," he said firmly, his voice steady despite the chaos surrounding him. They knew there was no convincing him otherwise.

He was one of thousands who sought refuge in public parks, pitching tents in whatever open spaces they could find. Families huddled under makeshift shelters, their eyes hollow with exhaustion and fear. One of the parks had been turned into a makeshift hospital, the air thick with the scent of antiseptic, blood, and sweat. Jun spent his days helping where he could- setting up tents for the displaced, offering quiet words of strength to those who had lost everything. But the worst was when he tried to pull people from the rubble.

The first time he dug through the debris, his fingers bled from gripping jagged cement, but he barely noticed. He strained to listen for voices beneath the wreckage, for any sign of life. Sometimes there were muffled cries, desperate hands reaching through cracks, and the frantic rush to pull someone free. Other times, there was only silence. Later, when Jun recounted those moments, his voice was flat, his eyes distant. "One old woman at the camp site held my hand and thanked me for helping pitch her tent. But I have never felt so helpless before," he admitted quietly. The look in his eyes told me that the smell of decay, the wails of grieving families, and the thought that he could have done more would stay with him for the rest of his life.

Rescue for those entombed by the collapsed structures took days, often stopped then resumed due to the many aftershocks. The longest rescue took 14 days. Among the first rescuers to arrive were miners from one of the gold mines in the province. With the roads impassable and the airport ruined, American and Philippine Air Force had to airlift supplies and aid to the people in Baguio City. In the aftermath, an estimated 1,621 people were killed in the affected areas including Baguio City.

It took a full month for the city and the universities to re-open. I got myself ready to go back to Baguio and as I reluctantly left my son behind in my mother's care, deep gratitude welled inside of me. The student strike may have saved me and countless other students. It was posited that there would have been more casualties if classes were in full swing in our university when the earth shook. I shuddered at that thought, I still do.

As the bus snaked its way up the winding road to Baguio, I wondered what laid ahead. I was imagining all sorts of scenario, and it made me anxious, I couldn't relax. As soon as we reached the first town up the mountain, a collective gasp echoed from inside the bus. The passengers, including me, were horrified by the damage unfolding in front of us. Half of the mountainside spilled over the roads to the ravines below. Half of the roads were gone; it was one way most of the way up. The guardrails, and hundreds of the houses dotting the mountainside were swallowed by the landslides. As I looked down, all I saw were deep ravines littered with flattened trees. It made me and the rest of the passengers nervous. I had to just keep looking forward.

The devastation in the city was gut-wrenching. Street after street looked like crumpled paper, the buildings reduced to broken concrete and twisted metal. Even the once-grand- five-star Hyatt Hotel had collapsed like a stack of pancakes. Private homes were decimated and many imposing buildings reduced to dust and rubble. The clean and sweet scent of pine that I love was replaced by the smell of dust and decay that permeated the air. I couldn't stop thinking about those trapped beneath the rubble- the ones who never made it, and those who somehow did, forever haunted by what they endured.

I pressed my hand against my mouth, willing myself not to cry, but the sheer scale of loss made it impossible to hold back.

As I walked toward the university, I saw a woman sitting outside the ruins of what used to be a bakery. She was cradling a framed photo to her chest, rocking back and forth. "It's all gone," she murmured to no one in particular. "Everything is gone."

I wanted to say something- anything- but what words could ease that kind of grief? I simply nodded in silent acknowledgment as I passed.

Later, I visited Nicole. Her house, though still standing, had deep cracks running along its walls. "We camped outside for days," she said, her voice trembling. "Every aftershock made us think it was happening all over again." She hesitated before adding, "You don't really sleep after something like that. You just close your eyes and wait for the earth to move again."

The sense of loss and despair in the eyes of those still living in tents on city parks pierced your soul, their homes either totally gone or have yet to be deemed structurally safe. Remember, these houses are built

201

on mountainsides. Mountainsides that have been shaken ferociously by the earthquake. Water supply was still intermittent with much of the water lines still being repaired. There was shortage of food and medical supplies. Some misguided souls have looted other people's homes and businesses. Unrest and uncertainty hung heavily in the air. This must be what war zones look like, I thought to myself.

Again and again, waves of emotions washed over me: gratitude for myself and my family, and sadness for those who lost property, homes and loved ones. And the realization that everything can be gone in an instant hit hard; everything is fleeting- the sense of security, happiness, love, and life. How does one plan for tomorrow when even today is daunting?

Yet, somehow, life had to go on. School reopened, and the steady rhythm of campus life returned, but I felt the tremors deep within me. Students trudged to and from class, but there was no excitement in their steps- no hurried chatter between friends. The empty seats in classrooms spoke louder than any announcement ever could. No one had to say it, but we all knew; many were lost, and those of us who remained felt guilty for continuing.

When I saw my friends again, we clung to each other as if the earth beneath our feet could still give way at any moment. Our laughter was quieter, more subdued. The joy was real, but the shadows of the disaster followed us, hovering like the ever-present threat of aftershocks.

Despite all the grief, despite the disquiet, we had to keep moving. We had to pass tests, turn in papers, and meet deadlines. Life went on because it had to. But there was a quiet, unspoken understanding among us: nothing could ever be the same. Not the city, not the people, not even ourselves. As I walked to my next class, I couldn't help but feel like every step forward was a betrayal to those we had lost- and to the very ground beneath our feet. The world moved on, and so did we.

Looking back now, that year taught me something sobering and profound: that no matter how much we plan or pray, we have no real control over the forces of nature. Mother Earth moves when she chooses- sudden, swift, without apology. All we can do is hold on, make the most of what we have while we have it, and hope the moment lasts longer than the tremor. And while we're here- while the ground is still beneath our feet- we try to leave it a little better than we found it.

But it wasn't just the earth that shifted. Something inside me moved too- cracked open by grief, by survival, by the recognition that aftershocks don't always come from the ground. Sometimes, they come from the heart. And those, too, leave fault lines we spend years trying to understand.

I wish I could say that the worst was behind me, that the ground beneath my feet had finally steadied. But life- like the earth- has its own fault lines, buried deep and hidden until they crack wide open.

I did not know it yet, but more tremors were coming. And some aftershocks do not just shake buildings- they shift everything you thought you knew about love, identity, and survival. And whether you are ready or not, you shift- and find a way to move with the tremors.

Chapter 16: Aftershocks

"She stood in the storm, and when the wind did not blow her way, she adjusted her sails."
  -Elizabeth Edwards

Some aftershocks are loud and violent, splitting the earth and rattling everything in their path. Others are quieter—lingering tremors that unsettle the heart long after the ground has stopped shaking.

In the months following the quake, the city and its citizens began the slow work of rebuilding. Workers were loading dump trucks with pieces of concrete, wood and steel, the dust swirling around them. It would take years to restore what had been lost. The destruction was massive-a brutal reminder of both nature's fury and the fragility of life. Most people stayed and worked to rebuild, while others chose to leave. Even the grand Hyatt Hotel was left in ruins, its empty shell rising above the city like a mausoleum of lost time.

I remember walking past it once on my way home from school. The sidewalk was cracked; a lamppost bent at a strange angle like it had knelt in prayer. There was silence in that part of town, an eerie stillness that pressed on my chest. A little girl in a pink dress stood beside her mother, staring at the crumbling building. "That used to be where people danced," the mother whispered. And then they moved on.

Despite the lingering devastation, life had to move forward. Classes resumed, and we all fell back into our routines. It felt strange, almost dissonant, to juggle assignments and exams while an entire city mourned. The makeshift tents in the parks, the scent of concrete dust still in the air- it was all still there, a reminder of how quickly everything could change.

But while the city was slowly healing, in my own life, the aftershocks were just beginning.

More than a year ago, my son's paternal family had moved from our small town to Baguio City as part of the patriarch's job promotion. When my son visited them, they'd take him in for a few days. His father- who was enrolled at an academy in the city- would occasionally stop by. Inevitably, our paths would cross.

At first, the meetings were awkward. A nod, a forced smile, a polite inquiry about our son's favorite food that week. But time has a funny way of softening hard edges. One afternoon, we ended up sitting side by side on a park bench as our son chased a paper airplane down the hill. He laughed so freely, his little arms stretched wide, believing he could fly. We shared a glance. A smile. And just like that, the door reopened.

At first, I told myself it was nothing- a few polite exchanges, an occasional shared laugh. But the past has a way of pulling you back in, especially when it's unfinished. I wanted to believe that maybe, just maybe, time had changed us. That the reckless love of our youth could mature into something real.

Even as I let myself be drawn in, a voice in the back of my mind whispered, "You know how this ends." I ignored it.

He began visiting more often. Sometimes I visited him at the academy. He introduced me to his classmates. They were kind, even warm- but when they learned we had a child together, I saw something flicker across their faces. Surprise. A quickly veiled awkwardness. Their curiosity was quiet but undeniable.

Then came the rumors- whispers passed through mutual friends. They said he was still seeing other women. That he may have fathered another child. I confronted him. He denied it. Swore it wasn't true. And every time he returned with a crooked smile and empty reassurance, I felt something inside me buckle. I wanted to believe him. I didn't want to be wrong about him again.

I even tried to coax an answer from his little sister, but she wouldn't say a word. I felt sorry after I asked her the question. She was just a young teenager- I shouldn't have put her on the spot. She also treated me like her older sister, which I was immensely grateful for. But her hesitation- her silence- said enough. I couldn't help but draw my own conclusion: he had fathered a child with someone else.

The heartbreak came back full force, and I felt like a fool for not listening to my instincts. My mother always reminded us while growing up:

"Your basic instincts are your first line of defense. If it feels weird, that's because it is weird. Run."

But once again, I didn't listen. And years later, my instincts proved right.

I tried to hide it, but Nicole and Mya could see how much I was suffering in silence. Once, we were back at Nicole's parents' house. We were sitting on the cool tile floor of Nicole's room; a bag of chips and half-melted ice cream between us, the fan spinning overhead. "What's going on?" Mya asked gently. I tried to hold it in, but the tears spilled anyway. Between sobs, I told them what I feared. I was grateful that they just listened. They didn't downplay nor inflame the situation. They just comforted and assured me that all will be well in the end. And I hoped in my heart that they were right.

Eventually, I had to admit two painful truths:

1. I was still in love with him.
2. I had become untouchable.

Where I came from, a woman with a child was seen as "spoiled goods." It didn't matter whether the man had remained loyal. The woman bore the scarlet letter. A mark that said, do not touch. Men distanced themselves. Even a whispered "Oooowww…" from a stranger could deliver the sting of judgment. Family members, too, reminded me of my "place."

So, when my classmates encouraged me to join the Miss Engineering contest- a lighthearted event meant to break the academic grind- I laughed it off. "You do know I have a child, right?" I said, half-joking. "I can't possibly be part of this."

But they insisted. "There's no rule that says you can't," one girl said. "You're smart, you're beautiful, and you're one of us." Eventually, I said yes. But beneath the surface, anxiety churned. I felt like I was walking into a lion's den.

On the night of the contest, the gymnasium buzzed with nervous energy. I slipped into a borrowed dress, my hands trembling as I applied eyeliner in the bathroom mirror. Behind me, one of the girls giggled. "Do we even know how to strut?" she joked. We laughed together, a brief moment of levity.

Backstage, a judge leaned in just enough to wound. "You shouldn't be here. You're not qualified. You have a son."

I had expected something like that. But it still cut deep. My cheeks burned. I nearly turned and walked away.

But then I thought: How long do I have to be punished?

I stayed. I stood on that stage, nervous at first. I caught a glimpse of one of my professors in the audience. He didn't smile. He didn't clap. Just watched with a face that said everything he didn't need to say. I almost turned back. Almost.

Then the crowd started cheering us on, and suddenly I felt that I belonged on that stage, any stage for that matter. So, I stood straighter, smiled and whispered to myself, "I am qualified- especially because I have a son."

I didn't win, but I didn't need to. Just being there, refusing to hide, was a small victory. A crack in the wall of shame they tried to build around me. As I walked back home alone, I started feeling giddy, almost delirious, I started laughing. "Oh my God! I actually did that!" I yelled in disbelief. And like a young child who got away with something, I skipped home with a smile on my face.

Looking back now, that contest taught me something about people- how tightly they cling to outdated beliefs, how fiercely they guard the boxes they've put us in.

Through all of it, Nicole and Mya were there. "Ignore the noise," Mya said once. "You'll be just fine." When I broke down one afternoon, Nicole brought me a bag of dried mangoes and sat beside me without saying a word. Sometimes, silence is the kindest kind of love.

I felt like I was running on a hamster wheel- chasing a future while being chased by a past I couldn't outrun. My grades slipped. I fell off the dean's list. I tried to stay focused; I still needed to keep my scholarship. But my drive was thinning, worn down by sleepless nights and heartbreak.

Yes, I held onto the scholarship, but the dream of graduating with honors slipped through my fingers. Again. It stung. But I reminded myself: You are still here. You are still standing.

Every time I felt myself sinking, I pictured my son's face- wide-eyed and full of trust. I'd remember how his fingers curled around mine, how he called me Mommy like it was the safest word he knew. He was my reason to fight.

There were days when the fog in my chest felt heavier than anything I'd carried during the quake. I kept thinking, "I've survived worse. I've walked through rubble. I've seen the sky fall." And yet, this kind of heartbreak- this quiet, private collapse- was colder than anything I'd known.

Sometimes, I imagined snow falling in a place like Baguio. Clean, quiet, soft. The kind that covers even broken things in a hush of grace. I longed for that kind of quiet- where the past didn't echo, and the future felt possible.

One day, I promised myself, I'll look back at this and say: look how far we've come.

I moved through the days like someone learning to breathe again- slowly, deliberately, one foot in front of the other. The earth had cracked beneath me, but I hadn't fallen through. Not this time. It also helped that Nicole and Mya were there to cheer me on when I started to shrink back. Their friendship made one of the toughest years in my life navigable.

There were still books to open, lessons to learn, promises to keep. And somewhere in the distance, the faint hum of something new was calling.

Then, quietly- like a dawn breaking after a storm- my final year arrived, five long years later.

And though there was no snow in Baguio, there was still something in the air- something crisp, something new. Maybe not a clean slate, but a softer ground to stand on. I was still standing. And somehow, that was enough.

Chapter 17: What Do You Want From Me?

"I have been bent and broken- but I hope into a better shape."
  -Charles Dickens, Great Expectations

My final year in college has arrived and I was looking forward to it. Not just for the reunions, but because the light at the end of the tunnel finally flickered into view. Everything I endured had led to this point. So, my siblings and I packed our bags and once again rode the bus back to Baguio City, each excited to continue our studies, each wondering how the year would unfold.

I was thrilled to see my college friends and classmates again. Some of them had stories of how their summer vacation went. Some spent so much time on the beaches they had turned several shades darker from the sun, their laughter light and carefree. There were no beach stories for me. Walking through the campus, I could hear excited chatter, laughter echoing in the corridors- a stark contrast to the heavy silence that followed me wherever I went as I was mostly pre-occupied by thoughts about finding work after college. Every smile and shared joke felt bittersweet, a reminder of the life I might have had if not for the heavy weight of my past decisions.

Amid the everyday grind of classes and the bittersweet reunions with friends, I sought refuge in my studies. I had always believed that knowledge could be my escape- a way to build a future that transcended the scars of my past. That conviction led me to choose a case study that would challenge me, one that forced me to confront the stark realities of the world around me.

A few days into the school year, one of our applied science classes required us to have a case study of our choosing. Whatever score we garnered from our case study would be 25% of our final grade before graduation. A lot was riding in these case studies! My class discussed what topics would be available to choose from. Determined to take the assignment seriously, I chose a topic that felt both challenging and unfamiliar, the oldest gold mine in the province.

Benguet province where my college town is located is known for gold deposits and had been a site of gold mining for centuries. In 1903, three Americans founded the Benguet Consolidated Mining Company, which later became the Benguet Corporation. It is one of the oldest and largest gold mining companies in the world.

My case study was about its history, technology, and processes. As part of my research, I gained access to their underground operation. It would be the first time I wore a hard hat with steel-toed boots. I was excited! With my guide, I was able to ride the tram all the way to about 300 ft underground. The descent was exhilarating. I was in awe of the feat that was accomplished, and slightly in fear of my unfamiliar surroundings. Being underground is just not normal.

But the deeper I went- both underground and into the company's history- the more troubling truths began to surface.

At first, the descent felt like an adventure. But that wore off quickly. The deeper we went, the colder and damper it became. The smell of exhaust fumes from the machinery was overpowering- surely toxic with long exposure. The stale scent of sweat lingered in the air, evidence of the long, brutal hours endured by the miners.

Even with the aid of machines, the labor was still backbreaking. I watched as workers maneuvered cumbersome, powerful equipment and, when it failed, hauled heavy rocks by hand. I realized then: this wasn't just a story about technology or process. It was about people. Exploited people.

As I wandered through the cold, damp corridors of the underground mine, the acrid exhaust fumes and the stifling heat of manual labor reminded me of the long, arduous days of my own struggles. The harsh conditions, the relentless work, and the systemic exploitation I learned about in my research echoed the challenges of a life built on sacrifice. In those dimly lit tunnels, I realized that, like the miners, I too was working under conditions not of my choice, battling forces far greater than myself.

I had newfound respect for the miners. They were not paid a lot of money, and I could see the exhaustion in their faces. But this is their job, whether by choice or necessity. Each of them needed to provide for their family, so they did their job day in and day out most of the time in less-than-ideal environment.

It took me almost a full semester to finish my case study. By the time I submitted it, I was exhausted- mentally, physically, emotionally. I handed it over to my instructor, who told me to wait for the results to be posted before the end of the semester.

During my research, I discovered that gold mining in Benguet was steeped in controversy. The mining corporations had displaced Indigenous communities and caused long-term damage to the environment and local agriculture. I hadn't considered these implications when I first chose the topic- I had been focused on the science, the process, the history. But the deeper I dug, the more sobering it became. I was confronted with how little I truly knew about the socio-economic realities shaping my own surroundings.

The more I examined the structures that kept these miners bound to hardship, the more I began to see how similar forces had shaped my own life. Religion. Shame. Silence. A life shaped by forces beyond my control, where the promise of a better future was constantly undermined by systemic neglect and exploitation.

See, as Catholics, we were told to abstain from sex, but no one talked about teenage hormones. Then there was the lack of access to contraceptives, because, once again, it was against our religion. No one ever explained things in a way that resonated with a young mind. We were shamed into not having sex, but was that ever effective with teenagers? The story from then to now, shows how ineffective that is.

Reading the statistics now is like looking into a mirror that reflected my own experience. Knowing that 24 babies per hour were born to Filipina girls between the ages of 10 and 19 made the isolation I felt even more poignant. It wasn't just a number- it was the story of countless lives marred by a system that shamed natural impulses and left young girls to bear the consequences of neglect. I see my own struggles in those figures, a reminder that my path was not unique but part of a heartbreaking cycle that continues to this day.

The injustices I uncovered in the mines weren't isolated- they were part of a wider pattern of neglect and exploitation. In much the same way, the shaming of young girls for natural instincts and the lack of proper guidance in matters of love and responsibility left many, including myself, struggling to find a voice.

Just as I was beginning to navigate the turbulent landscape of my academic and personal life, nature itself reminded me of its capricious power. When I looked up and saw tiny flakes drifting from the sky like snow, it felt as though the heavens themselves were crying out- a portent of the chaos that was about to engulf us once again.

Mount Pinatubo, a long-dormant volcano, had erupted, sending a massive ash cloud across the country. Towns and villages were buried under layers of volcanic debris. Roofs caved in under the weight of the wet ash, killing hundreds. Thousands more lost their homes.

A couple of my classmates had family there- thankfully, they were able to evacuate. But their homes were gone, buried beneath ash and debris. The devastation stretched for years, as rain turned the ash into thick, merciless mudflows.

Months later, I saw it with my own eyes: entire towns erased, highways rebuilt on layers of hardened lava. Church steeples and rooftops jutted out from the ground like strange monuments, the rest of the buildings swallowed by the earth.

The US bases- Subic Bay and Clark- were rendered inoperable. The Americans cut their losses and left.

Not again. The same hopelessness I felt after the earthquake came rushing back. How much more could we endure?

Sometimes I wondered if we were just like beavers, forever rebuilding our dams, knowing the flood will come again. The beauty of this country is also its curse. We sit on the Ring of Fire- where the earth never truly rests.

Looking back now, I think that was the first time I ever felt truly helpless- when even breathing felt futile. The enormity of what we were facing made everything else feel small, meaningless. I remember wondering: Why keep going, when nothing I do seems to make a difference? What good strength is if it can't protect the ones you love or stop the ground from breaking beneath your feet?

Have you ever felt pain so raw that it takes over your body? That night, as the ash cloud swallowed the sky and the relentless rain turned the world into a blur of gray, something in me shattered. I curled into myself, hugging my knees, gasping for breath between sobs. The air was thick with sulfur and silence.

Sobbing into the darkness, as if the night might answer back, I begged, 'What do you want from me?' It wasn't anger. It was despair, bone-deep and aching. But then, somewhere between the tears and the silence, something shifted. Not in the world- but in me.

"I surrender," I whispered. Not in defeat, but in faith. A letting go. And later, when the ache returned, I said again, louder this time. "I am done fighting. Thy will be done. I surrender."

I had nothing left.

The sobbing slowed. I could breathe again- not easily but enough. The fog in my mind lifted. The ache remained, but it no longer crushed me. I had spent years asking why, trying to hold on to something that was never meant to be. That night, I let it go.

My arms slacked. My breath steadied. I surrendered to Him, and I surrendered him.

In hindsight, that night planted something in me- a deeper kind of strength, forged not by fighting, but by releasing what I couldn't control. It would be a strength I'd return to many times in the years to come, when the ground shook again- metaphorically and otherwise. Because some storms you endure, and others… you outlast by trusting that the sun will rise, even if you can't yet see the light.

In the days that followed, as I felt the heavy burden of my past gradually lift, I began to see a path forward- not one free of pain, but one illuminated by the lessons learned from every trial. The shattered fragments of my past were being pieced together by the love of my family, the memories of those who had endured before me, and the unyielding hope that no matter how dark the night, a new dawn will always come.

My mother would often share how Mark was thriving- bright, observant, full of curiosity. They lived in our little house on the hill, where Mark often tagged along with my mother to her classroom, eager to be near her. One day while my mother was checking schoolwork, he asked Mom for a snack, and she only had bread at that time. Mark, it seemed, didn't like the type of bread. As we have already established, my mother had a different way of instilling lessons. She told my son that if he didn't like the bread, he could give it away to his friends. Mark left with the bread and moments later, he was back in my mother's classroom, empty-handed.

"Where's your bread?"

"Lola, you said to give it away to my friends, so I did." Mark responded.

My mother said it took every ounce of her not to show herself laughing and amused.

It was moments like this that made life's challenges bearable. My son's kind nature, and also his ability to stand his ground- he didn't like it, so he didn't eat it- gave so much sunshine in my sometimes-overcast world. And of course, my mother's core as a teacher- every moment is a chance to shape, to mold, to instill lessons that one can carry through life- as she had done with me and my siblings.

In a world where so much felt beyond my control- nature, systems, expectations- it was the small, unguarded moments that brought me back to myself. Mark's innocence, his literal heart, reminded me that life still held lightness. That even in a landscape scorched by loss and disappointment, something tender could grow. And maybe that's what kept me going-the quiet, unexpected graces tucked inside the chaos.

Maybe that night, the answer to my question wasn't thunderous, but quiet- woven into the hush of rain, the soft rise and fall of my breath. What do You want from me? The echo, once raw and aching, softened into something almost sacred. Maybe what was asked of me wasn't perfection or unshakable strength, but the willingness to feel, to endure, to surrender- and still choose to love. Maybe what was asked... was to keep going, to soften where I had hardened, to make space for grace.

And maybe, just maybe, the answer came not with thunder, but in a small, radiant moment- when my son gave away his bread without question, simply because his Lola told him he could. In that act, so innocent and sure, was everything I had been trying to reclaim- faith, kindness, trust. What do You want from me?

Perhaps... exactly that.

"Though the earth trembles, my spirit does not break. I am held by something deeper."

Chapter 18: Where the Road Bends

"There are years that ask questions and years that answer."
  -Zora Neale Hurston

After the storm of surrender came the quiet life of rebuilding. Life moved forward, and so did I. I earned a degree in Electronics & Communications Engineering. The biggest employer in my college town at that time was Texas Instruments (TI). Everybody is familiar with their scientific calculator, but not everybody is aware that it was and still is one of the biggest manufacturers of integrated circuits, or IC chips. They came to our college looking to recruit soon to be graduates as interns in their On-the-Job (OJT) Training Program. I was one of the fortunate ones to be selected. The following month after graduation, I started my training at Texas Instruments.

I didn't have a car then, so I took the company bus from a designated area in the city to their location. We had to pass through a security gate to enter the compound. The TI compound was nestled in the rolling hills of Baguio, its modern facade contrasting with the lush pine-dotted landscape. Entering the massive main building for the first time, I felt a mix of awe and determination. The slogan "Do it right the first time" was emblazoned on the wall- a mantra that would be drilled into us throughout our training.

The Gold Bond area- where microscopic gold wires are bonded to chips to create electrical connections was our first training ground. It is a cleanroom- a controlled environment that filters out pollutants to create a clean space. Cleanrooms are used in many industries including pharmaceuticals, biotechnology and, in this case, electronics manufacturing. Walking into the cleanroom felt like stepping into another world. Every precaution was taken to ensure absolute cleanliness. The airlock hissed as I passed through, the powerful filtration system blasting away any stray particles. My smock, gloves, and hairnet felt alien at first, but soon they became part of the routine. The cleanroom was sterile and quiet, with only the faint hum of machinery breaking the silence. The smock felt awkward and stifling at first, but I soon came to see it as a badge of my new career.

The "gold bond area" on an integrated circuit (IC) refers to a designated pad or region on the chip where a gold wire is precisely bonded to establish an electrical connection, typically using a process called "wire bonding" which utilizes the high conductivity and corrosion resistance of gold to create reliable connections between the chip and its package pins; essentially, it's the specific spot on the IC where a gold wire is attached to make a connection to another component. Gold is the primary material used due to its excellent electrical conductivity and resistance to oxidation.

We trained on the processes and procedures and on the machines involved in "gold bonding".

The next training was at the test area where, as the name implies, the IC chips were tested using dedicated machines. They were evaluated to see if they are functioning as they were designed to do. This area wasn't a cleanroom, thank goodness. I liked the test area. It was where

I applied some of my college education. I read schematic diagrams, repaired mother boards, and entered programs into the machine.

I was quietly grateful for how different this environment was from the life I had known the past few years. Where there was uncertainty, there is now precision. Where there was hopelessness, there are now results. And where there was chaos, now a sense of calm.

When I was hired full-time, I was placed in the Gold Bond area, not in the test area where I wanted to be. Still, I felt proud to have earned a spot in a global company like TI. But the pride quickly turned to frustrations. I realized that my male counterparts- graduates from the same class, part of the same training program- were hired as engineers, while I, a woman, was given the title of technician.

I asked one of my trainers why. She sighed, her expression unreadable. "That's the way it has always been done." Her voice carried a hint of frustration, but not at me- at the system, at the unspoken rule she had likely faced herself. A rule that, despite her years in the industry, she had not been able to change.

There it was again: my place. A woman's place. The invisible boundary drawn not by merit but by tradition. Even though TI was an American company, it conformed to the country's outdated gender roles. I swallowed the injustice, just as countless women before me had, and focused on what I could control: I had a stable job, and soon, my son would be with me.

But the sting of that moment never fully faded. It settled deep, shaping the way I would see the workplace, the questions I would ask, the battles I would choose to fight. Because once you recognize inequality-

once you feel it firsthand- you never unsee it.

Just as I was beginning to learn how to navigate these invisible ceilings, life surprised me with something I hadn't expected- a partner who saw me beyond my job title. I was introduced to a visiting engineer, Dan, from Massachusetts. The older ladies I worked with warned me about the expats. Expats are playboys, they said. It turned out this expat wasn't. Even his Filipino guy friends vouched for him. "He's from Massachusetts so he is not like the expats from Dallas." They said.

"How exactly are the expats from Dallas like?" I asked, confused and curious at the same time. "Oh, you know, they are loud and like to drink and visit strip clubs." One of them said.

I was amused, but that was my first education in expats, and by extension, regional cultures in the US.

Dan and I hit it off, and he didn't care that I was "untouchable", he thought it was ridiculous. A gentleman through and through, he treated me with respect and tenderness. More importantly, he loved me unconditionally and accepted me with all the baggage that came with me, my son, and my family. Though he didn't see them as a baggage, more like a blessing. When he asked me to marry him, I said yes.

Leaving work a few days later, we were in his car, and he was driving. I told him that he needed to provide a pig to my family per tradition for our engagement. "A pig!" He exclaimed almost swerving the car off the road. I explained why. He joked, "So all I need to get your father's blessing is a pig. I can afford that!" It is a story he relished telling his

American family. He found this cultural tradition endearing in a way. Perhaps because his mother is an immigrant herself, he understood.

I decided to have the wedding in the city to spare him from the tradition and expectation of a big wedding back in the province. For weddings there, the invitation is open. Meaning, the invited guests have their own invited guests. So, a wedding planned for 100 guests can easily end up being 300 or more guests.

The day of the wedding was beautiful. The sun was shining bright, and the flowers everywhere were in full bloom. My son Mark is the ring bearer, and he proudly and protectively cradled the small white pillow that held the rings.

"Don't touch it!" He snapped at anyone who tried to examine the rings, "You'll tarnish the shine!"

My sister Bugsy, my maid of honor, and I were getting our hair and makeup done, the stylists working their magic to make us feel beautiful.

There was a knock on the door. It was Dan and his best man, looking sheepish in their suits. "We have to go pick up the wedding cake from the bakery." Dan said.

"What? Now?"

"Yes. They don't deliver, apparently." And off they went.

My sister and I looked at each other. "Seriously?" my sister said, exasperated. It became the running joke of the day.

We ended up with 350 people. The restaurant where the reception was kept adding tables as more guests arrived. Some guests arrived in buses, braving the eight-hour trek one way. Many I knew, some I didn't recognize, but all came to celebrate. They mingled, ate and danced the night away, then boarded the bus back to the province.

I was glad they came. I had finally shared something beautiful with them- something I was proud of. For one perfect day, perhaps they didn't see a teenager who got pregnant- a cautionary tale- but a woman who had persevered and rose above the weight of judgment. And that gave me a deep sense of peace.

One of Dan's sisters, Paula, flew from the US to attend the wedding. I didn't expect any of his family to come, it's almost a full day of travel. So, I was delighted when she told us she was flying in. She was great! She was curious and open to the eccentricities and uniqueness of my country. She found the people kind and the food great. "I love the mangoes here! I can eat them all day and every day." She said, excitedly.

I spoke with Dan's parents over the phone. They were so warm in their tone. They welcomed me to the family and apologized for not attending because the husband just had a triple bypass surgery. I told them I understood. I was grateful, even relieved, that they are welcoming.

Dan and I planned our honeymoon to Boracay, one of the famous islands in the Philippines, for its resorts and beautiful beaches. I didn't want Paula to stay in Baguio alone, so we invited her to join us. "Are you sure?" She asked, amazed that I am including her. "Of course!" I said. I didn't mind at all. I appreciated that she took the time and energy to attend the wedding. Plus, Boracay is beautiful, and it is more beautiful when shared with family.

Several months later, I bore Dan a son who we named after his father. We nicknamed him Rence, short for Lawrence. Dan's father was so happy that we named his newest grandson after him. Unfortunately, he would never meet his namesake; he passed away three months later. I was glad that before he passed, he knew his legacy would live on through his grandson we named after him.

As we were settling into the rhythm of our new life, we encountered an old shadow from my past- a battle I didn't expect to fight. My husband decided to adopt my first born, Mark, who was so excited to finally have a regular father figure in his life! As my husband prepared to adopt Mark, Mark's biological father challenged the process. He hadn't been regularly involved in our son's life, but perhaps out of pride or a need for control, he refused to make it easy. Four hearings were scheduled, and four times he did not show up. Each time, I sat in that courtroom, heart in my throat, hoping for resolution. Finally, the judge ruled in our favor. When the papers were signed, it wasn't just a legal victory- it was the moment my son truly gained the father he had longed for. Watching them together, I knew, without a doubt, that this was meant to be.

With our family finally united under one name, we started welcoming more pieces of the puzzle. My mother-in-law visited us and met her grandsons for the first time. "Great to meet you." She said in her high-pitched voice as she gave me a big hug. She was a Russian immigrant, a war bride, and she had a commanding presence. I suppose she had to be. Her late husband was in the military and together they had seven children, born in various places where he was stationed. She had for the most part raised those children by herself. And she raised kind responsible children. She impressed me.

I don't know what I expected but she was a loving woman. She treated my first born like she did my second, her own blood. Whatever trepidations or worry I had were immediately put to rest.

My husband and I talked about eventually having to move to the US with him once his assignment in TI Philippines was over. In the meantime, he still had to travel back and forth to the US. He wanted us to travel with him so we thought it would be a good idea for me to apply for a visitor's visa instead of an immigrant visa since we won't be living in the US for at least another 3 years. So, with our sons Mark and Rence in tow, we drove the 8-hour drive from Baguio City to Manila to file for my visitor's visa at the American Embassy.

I was denied the visitor's visa. I was stunned! It felt like a door I had been so sure would open had suddenly slammed shut. The frustration wasn't just about the bureaucracy- it was about the helplessness of knowing my plans for my family had to be delayed yet again. The visa denial was a bitter pill to swallow. The logic seemed backward: I was eligible to emigrate, yet I couldn't visit? As we drove back to Baguio, my mind raced with questions. What would this mean for my family? How much longer would we have to wait?

Mark looked at me, confused. "So... we're not going with Daddy?" he asked. I smiled through gritted teeth, masking the sting. "Not yet," I said," But soon."

Before we left the embassy, we were advised that for my interview for the immigrant visa, we had to bring our marriage certificate, and any other documents we had, to prove that we were legally married. They also told us to bring any letters or cards that we sent to each other to show that our marriage wasn't a marriage of convenience. Nice!

I eventually had my interview. The consul who was also my interviewer led me to his office. It was nondescript. Except for the consul's personal items, a picture of his family, a paperweight with his name on it, it was just like any other government office. The consul was all business; it felt like an interrogation! "How did you meet?" "Did you live together before you got married?" "Where did you get married?" "Was it by a priest or by a government official?"

He wondered why we didn't have any letters to each other. Because we worked together and there was email! The questions were infuriating. In the meantime, my youngest son kept crawling into the interview room! Is he not proof enough that my marriage is not a marriage of convenience? Good God!

I did finally get my immigrant visa—whew!

For the first time in my life- and my oldest son's- we took our very first flight to the United States. Rence was barely a year old then, so he doesn't remember anything. But I remember stepping out of TF Green International Airport in Providence, Rhode Island that December- and I was beyond cold. We don't have winters in the Philippines, so this was a shock to my system.

From the airport, we went straight to the mall to buy winter coats for me, Mark, and Rence. Mark was in awe. The mall was the biggest store he had ever seen, and it was packed with holiday shoppers. His eyes were wide with wonder, and I could tell he was amused. He grabbed my hand.

"Too many people, Mom," he said, smiling.

"I know, right?" I replied quietly.

I was amazed at the sheer frenzy of Christmas shopping. The mall was a madhouse—people pushing carts through crowded aisles, long lines at every cashier, babies in strollers, toddlers crying, parents juggling bags and frustration. I just wanted a warm winter coat, I thought wryly.

Warm and bundled in our new jackets, we finally drove to Dan's house in Rhode Island. It was a modest ranch-style home in a quiet, tree-lined neighborhood. I peered out the window at the empty street, the houses glowing softly in the early winter dark.

Maybe everyone's already tucked in for the night, I thought.

Or maybe this kind of stillness was just normal here.

The bitter cold nipped at our skin the moment we stepped out of the car. I scooped up the children and rushed them inside, grateful that Dan had already unlocked the front door. The warmth hit me instantly-dry, steady, unfamiliar. For the first time in my life, I smelled the heat. We never had heaters growing up, not even in our big apartment back in Baguio. This was a treat, a comfort, a small luxury I never knew to dream of. "Nice!" Mark said, running his hand across the plush couch before sinking into it, his voice full of wonder.

I smiled. I couldn't help but think of everything it had taken to get here- from cramped teacher's quarters to this quiet home in America, warmed by both a thermostat and dreams I once thought was out of reach. The road had bent in ways I never could have predicted. But here we were- warm, safe, and home.

"Mom, wake up! It's snowing!" Mark shouted the next morning, his voice cutting through the quiet like a bell.

I blinked, then sat up quickly. "It is?" I asked, matching his excitement.

We hurried to the living room window and stood together, side by side, staring in awe. Outside, snow fell in slow, graceful spirals, blanketing the yard in white. Mark's face was lit with amazement, his breath fogging the glass.

"Wow! Can I go outside and play in it?"

So, I bundled him up- his brand-new winter coat, boots, scarf, gloves, and a little hat pulled snug over his ears. I watched from the window as he stepped into the snow, cautious at first, then thrilled. He scooped up handfuls and tossed them into the air, laughing as they fell back down like feathers. His joy was radiant, unfiltered, the kind of joy that made time stand still.

I stood there, my hand resting on the cold glass, and felt something settle inside me. It wasn't long ago that I was consumed by survival- just trying to graduate, trying to find a job, trying to keep us afloat. Back then, playing in the snow felt like a distant fantasy meant for someone else's life. And yet, here we were.

That morning, watching Mark dance in the snow, I realized: we didn't just survive. We crossed oceans, defied odds, and made it to this moment. This snow-covered morning in a quiet American suburb was proof. Not of perfection, but of progress. Of how far we had come.

We spent our first Christmas with Dan's family. It was the first time I met most of his siblings – he has three sisters and three brothers-, their partners, and children. I wasn't sure what to expect - new faces, new customs, maybe a bit of awkwardness. But there was none of that. Only warmth. They welcomed me and my children with open arms. Mark especially seemed at ease, laughing and playing with his new cousins like he had known them forever. Watching him, so happy and unguarded, nearly brought tears to my eyes. Beyond our family back home, he had found another. And so had I.

We visited another time after that, but Dan still had two years left on his expat contract, so we made the decision to stay in the Philippines for two more years. I was also then pregnant with my third child, so it seemed like a no brainer decision.

For the first time in a long time, everyone seemed to be where they were supposed to be. My parents were living in our province; my father decided to retire while my mother stayed a schoolteacher. Her accident a distant memory and her children are thriving, so she was content. My brother Jun, having graduated with a degree in Education, found a job as a high school teacher then eventually with the provincial government as a Local Government Operations Officer, or simply a Field Officer.

Jun loved being a Field Officer. With that role, he had the chance to work in the Cordillera Region provinces. He worked with local government officials, employees and community leaders in the areas of local governance, peace & order and public safety, and community empowerment. His role encompassed government administration, infrastructure projects, socio-economic programs, and community organization capability building, among others, for the remotest and poorest barangays. (Barangays are the smallest local government units in the Philippines.)

My youngest brother Chris by now was a freshman in college. He followed us, his older siblings, and enrolled at St Louis University, majoring in engineering, as I did. I can remember how wide-eyed and excited he was to be in the same city as the rest of us. We got him a small place near the university. With my sister Bugsy living with me and my growing family, we thought it would be too much of an imposition on my new husband if he also lived with us.

He was gifted in music and the guitar was his instrument of choice. We would go watch him play at local music venues. He had a natural gift for performing live, and his smile- broad, infectious- lit up every room. Watching him on stage was pure joy. In a different life, he would have probably formed a band and toured. In this life, he studied to become an engineer. A practical choice.

Our parents always encouraged us to go after our dreams and not to settle. And I don't think they would have discouraged him if he chose a life in music. But he announced that he was choosing engineering as his major, and no one questioned it.

Sometimes I wished that I had talked to him more- to really understand his dreams. But I was too busy putting my life back together, too wrapped up in surviving, to notice the quiet distance growing between us. We were only seven years apart, but life had pulled those years in opposite directions.

232

My sister Bugsy was in the thick of her pre-med studies. She was living with us so she doesn't have to pay rent, in turn she can help with the kids. With my job, I was able to help pay her tuition.

Upon learning of this arrangement, one of my aunts on my father's side asked if I could help send her second eldest daughter Jen through college. I thought about it long and hard. I didn't want my husband's generosity and kindness taken advantage of. He also was from a different culture and tradition so I didn't know if he would understand. In my province, it is an unspoken tradition for the oldest child in the family to take care of the younger ones, which includes sending them to school. I was already sending my sister through pre-med and eventually, medical school. Did I really want to take on another responsibility?

I discussed the request with my husband, who true to form, said he was fine with me helping my cousin Jen. I spoke with my mother about it who said it was my decision, but I shouldn't feel obligated.

There is a fine line between giving generously and giving guiltily, and I was straddling the fine line. I felt blessed and grateful to finally make money and be able to help family. I also felt guilty if I didn't help. Years later I would learn the phrase "Catholic Guilt". In Catholic doctrine, guilt is often associated with the acknowledgment of sin and the recognition of one's moral transgressions. This feeling of guilt is seen as a positive force that can lead individuals to seek forgiveness, make amends, and strive for moral improvement. It can also be detrimental to mental health if it causes imbalance in one's psyche.

I agreed to help Jen. I told her she could live with us and help with the chores; in turn I would send her though trade school. She agreed.

Was my decision to help her part of me making amends for my earlier transgressions? Perhaps. Was I paying it forward? Absolutely.

After Jen finished trade school, her mother approached me again. She asked if I could send her other daughter Ellen through school.

I was flabbergasted. More like shocked really. The audacity, I thought. Does she really expect me to put all her children through school? I quietly said no. "Jen can now pay it forward as I did." I walked away from that conversation seething. Was my aunt trying to take advantage of me? Was she even grateful for what I did for my cousin, her daughter? I told my mother how I felt. "You have to forgive your aunt. She doesn't know any better." My mother said.

That conversation made me evaluate the customs and traditions I grew up with. There were so many good things about them; respect for the elders, the feeling of community with family helping family, the oldest members helping the young. But I couldn't help but think how these can be abused. It can put a tremendous amount of burden on the person helping, especially financially. And it can inadvertently be enabling to those receiving the help. I couldn't help but think, was I inadvertently enabling my aunt?

The Filipino culture in general is steeped with customs and traditions, passed on from one generation to another. Some of them are treasures, a few of them we can do without. By nature, Filipinos are happy go lucky people. We are known for laughing at the face of poverty. The happiest poor people, most foreigners say. But there is also the other side of us. We can be judgmental without meaning to be and are great at giving double edged compliments.

234

I remember an incident after my son Rence was born. I brought him to one of the work functions when he was barely walking. One of my co-workers was gushing over him. "Oh, my goodness, he is so cute! So handsome! But he doesn't look like you!" She exclaimed.

I smiled and said thank you.

Over time I decided that I would take all the good things I learned from these customs and traditions and throw away what doesn't serve me. The good ones, I will pass on to my children.

Mark, my oldest, was by then in second grade. He was enjoying his new school and found new friends. He was a doting and proud big brother to Rence. You can see it in his beautiful smile when he spoke to his little brother. They loved the outdoors! We took them to the nearby parks often where they enjoyed riding on ponies and running around like kids do. Watching them carefree and having so much fun reminded me a little bit of my carefree childhood. I smiled at those memories, I still do.

Just when I thought all is finally well, and the road would stay straight, life reminded me who was really behind the wheel- and it wasn't me. The path bent sharply, sending me through hairpin turns and sudden drops, stirring emotions so deep and profound they could render even the strongest person helpless.

But the truest tests of strength weren't in classrooms or boardrooms. They were still to come- inside the walls of my own home.

Chapter 19: Splinters and Sutures

"To be a mother is to have your heart go walking around outside your body."

-Elizabeth Stone

A broken bone, a fractured plan, and a new beginning stitched together by love, lessons, and letting go.

My two-year-old Rence- who climbed trees, jumped like a cat, and ran like his life depended on it- was suddenly crawling again. And each time we forced him to stand up and walk, he would hold on to the wall and cry in pain. That went on for a few days. We took him to the pediatrician who couldn't find anything wrong with him. She suggested we should have him undergo a scan.

The scan showed a hairline fracture on his left femur just under his hips. It also showed a mass next to the hairline fracture. The doctor explained that the fracture was what was causing the pain, and the mass made the bone around it porous, causing the hairline fracture. "I am afraid the mass is a tumor, but I am not certain. You need to bring him to an orthopedic surgeon." The doctor said, matter-of-factly.

My husband and I were shocked in disbelief. We went home in silence.

I locked myself in the bathroom, not wanting my children to see me cry with worry and uncertainty. That night was the longest night in my life. Dan and I discussed what the next steps are. He wanted the best doctors to determine what was wrong, so we decided that we needed to fly to the US right away.

The following morning, Dan called his sister Paula. She was a physical therapist so she would know the best hospitals and best doctors for this. We told her that the doctor in Baguio wasn't sure if it was a tumor, and she advised us not to research online, or it would drive us crazy. After a few days, Paula called back and informed us that she was able to schedule an appointment with an orthopedic surgeon at the Massachusetts Children's Hospital in Boston, one of the best in the country.

One week after the scan, we packed our bags, left everything else behind and boarded the plane to the United States, uncertain of what lies ahead. Mark, 9 years old by then, helped cheer up his brother Rence who refused to be on his feet at all, perhaps afraid of the ensuing pain. I was seven months pregnant and extremely uncomfortable. Dan tried to keep everything together. It was the longest flight of my life.

We arrived at night, went to the house, and barely slept. Early that following morning, we dropped off Mark at Dan's sister Claire's house, then drove to Boston.

The building was beautiful. In the receiving hall, there was a contraption for perpetual motion, where a ball was continuously moving, snaking its way through tubes and tunnels. But its beauty could not mask the sterile smell, nor could it cover the grim look on some faces. I couldn't help but wonder what they were there for.

We approached the registration tables, filled out all the paperwork and were directed to the surgeon's office, all the while moving like robots, mindless. Dr Gertz welcomed us to the office. We gave him a quick summary of what happened and handed him the note from the doctor in Baguio. He studied the notes quietly, then spoke quietly. "We will do an MRI right away so we can figure out what we are dealing with." He said, warm and reassuring, and yet distant.

They wheeled Rence away. We followed- silent, hollow, afraid. The technicians had to manipulate his leg to get a good MRI result, and each time they did that, we could hear Rence screaming in agony. It broke our hearts to hear him scream. I wish I could take all that pain away. I cried quietly, as I held on to Dan while he tried to be strong for both of us.

For what felt like a lifetime, Dr Gertz finally appeared. He sat us down and gave us the good news and bad news. I braced myself. "Good news, he doesn't have a cancerous tumor." I let out a deep sigh. My husband and I looked at each other, relieved. "What is the bad news?" I heard him say.

Dr Gertz explained that Rence had a unicameral bone cyst. A unicameral, or simple, bone cyst is a common, benign (noncancerous) bone tumor that primarily occurs in children and adolescents. Unicameral bone cysts (UBC) are cavities within bone that are filled with fluid. Although they can develop in any bone, UBCs usually affect the long bones- most often the upper arm bone (humerus) and the thighbone (femur).

In most cases, unicameral bone cysts are not painful and are often discovered incidentally when an X-ray is obtained for another reason.

Because these cysts can weaken the surrounding bone, fractures through UBCs do occur. Treatment for a UBC is based on several factors, including the size and location of the cyst, and the risk for fracture. In some cases, surgery may be recommended.

Cyst. The word sounded harmless. But not in a bone. Not in my baby.

Dr. Gertz went on to say that before they can treat the cyst, the fracture had to be addressed first. He added that because the cyst was located at the top of the left femur, Rence had to be put in a body cast from his ribs all the way down to the left ankle, and to above the knee of the right leg, with a hole in the crotch area to make way for his bodily functions. He will be in the body cast for 4 weeks, to give time for the fracture to heal and the bones to strengthen a little. That meant Rence would be back in a diaper for that duration as well.

Dan and I listened. We were thankful that the tumor wasn't cancerous, and at the same time, we were almost suspended as the words slowly sunk in. Dr Gertz' words seem to be coming from far away, "Do you understand what I am saying?" Yes, I nodded meekly. "Once the fracture is healed, we will perform an aspiration to remove the fluid from the bone, then we will fill it with steroid and calcium to aid the thickening of the bones. Hopefully, that will fix the problem. If not, then we will discuss the next steps."

I could barely hear the conversation between Dan and Dr Gertz, but I could see their mouths moving. Suddenly, we were ushered once again to the waiting room as Rence was fitted his body cast. I could hear his wails and once again, the feeling of helplessness consumed me.

After what seemed like forever, we were led to the casting room. Rence was asleep, exhausted, his dry tears caked on his face. Looking at him, I felt the now familiar pain deep in the pits of my stomach, as I tried to push the tears away. Was it maternal guilt? Terror? Was it the unbearable reality of watching your child immobilized? The attendant sat us down and informed us that we needed to keep the cast clean to protect the skin. He showed us how to line the inside of the cast around the crotch area with plastic to prevent the bodily fluids from seeping into the rest of the cast. Then, fit an adult diaper over it. I was overwhelmed, I couldn't think. I shook my head, trying to absorb the information, I needed to keep a clear head.

It was late in the afternoon when Rence was discharged. Dr Gertz reassured us that the worse was over. "We now know what we are dealing with. Bring him back here in a month for the aspiration procedure."

With that, Dan lifted Rence from the bed and strapped him in the stroller. The stroller had to be adjusted to almost flat because Rence could not sit up, he had to lay down, his head and upper body propped by a pillow, the body cast rigid around his waist up to his ribs.

We walked to the car, dazed. The entire day was a blur, but it wasn't. My mind was running amuck. I was seven months pregnant with a two-year old in a body cast. This is going to be a challenge, I thought.

It was dark by the time we got home. Claire dropped off Mark. We informed her of the diagnosis. Relieved that it was not cancerous, she gave us a hug and left as we settled in. Mark was curious about the body cast, so we explained to him as simply as we could what the diagnosis was and what laid ahead.

The first few days felt like triage. We enrolled Mark in the nearby elementary school so he wouldn't miss any more classes; Dan was working in the Massachusetts TI plant; I spent hours on tearful phone calls with mom- "You are a strong woman, "she'd whisper- until even I believed it. And all the while, Rence, back in diapers and in a body cast, was taking it all in stride.

Remarkably, Rence was resilient and in great spirits. He learned how to walk with that body cast! He would prop himself up from the floor using a sturdy chair, couch or wall. Then he would use his right leg as a fulcrum to swing his cast covered left leg, place his left foot down then alternating those actions, he walked. We had large bean bags in the living room and in his room where he would just plop himself down.

He could walk fast in that cast! I'd yell, "Careful- don't miss the beanbag!" And he'd beam at me, racing across the room, proof that resilience can look like pure unbridled joy. When he would hear his father's car pull up after a workday, he would bounce right up and be the first at the door. "Hi, dad!" then proceeded to tell his father how his day went.

He loved playing hide and seek with some of the children in the neighborhood. Of course, he couldn't hide well because of the bulkiness of his body cast, but that didn't stop him. He didn't mind being the "it" most of the time. He would laugh and run whenever he found someone.

His big brother Mark would help him hide, sometimes covering his exposed left leg with twigs and leaves. It was funny to watch.

My sons adjusted well to the situation, but I couldn't wait for the month to be over, hoping and praying at the same time that the fracture in Rence's femur has healed so we can go to the next step. We busied ourselves getting the baby's room ready; we applied a fresh coat of paint and assembled the new crib. Still, the month seemed to drag on and when it finally arrived, we anxiously made our way back to the hospital, hopeful. After the cast was split open, Rence was once again wheeled to the MRI room. Dan and I were anxious for the result.

Dr Gertz delivered the good news.

"The fracture has been healed. We are now going to administer anesthesia then aspirate the bone cyst."

He introduced us to the hospital family liaison who informed us that the procedure would take a while, and that Rence had to be under observation for a while. He connected us with the Ronald McDonald house down the street, where we can make ourselves comfortable while waiting.

The Ronald McDonald Houses are run by the Ronald McDonald House Charities RMHC. It is an independent nonprofit organization that help families stay close to their child when they need treatment for serious condition. The Houses provide a home-like setting, close to the region's top hospitals, where families can stay free of charge for as long as necessary.

We reluctantly left the hospital- still smelling of disinfectant. We didn't know what to expect, only that we needed to breath. What we found down the street softened something in us. As we stepped into RMHC's Victorian warmth, we were greeted by the hush of chattering parents, the sweet scent of baking cookies, the threadbare armchairs that seemed to say, "Stay as long as you need."

A volunteer walked out from the kitchen and welcomed us. She was a middle-aged woman who told us that she was baking cookies. She gave us a tour of the house. It had several bedrooms and most of them were occupied. She explained to us that we could have our own bedroom if we needed one. Luckily, we didn't need to. Rence will be discharged later that day. We just needed a place to relax while waiting.

As Mark raced off to play with some of the kids, I watched the other children- the chemotherapy-bald and the wheelchair-bound- and felt my petty worries shrink. In their courage, I recognized a family's fiercest truth: we are at our strongest when we lean on each other. And so, in that cozy living room, I found myself breathing easier than I had in weeks.

It was almost dark when Dr Gertz called. "Rence did great, and he is ready to go home."

Rence was smiling when we entered the room. His cast was now split in two so he can get out of it when necessary. His left leg was atrophied, so skinny compared to his right leg.

"Look! My cast has belts now." He said excitedly, referring to the 3 straps on the cast: one to go around the waist, and one for each leg.

Dr Gertz explained it was now a wait and see. "You have to bring him back in 6 months for an MRI."

We went home, exhausted, but relieved. Relieved because there were other children and families in much worse circumstances. As we were leaving the hospital, I couldn't help but feel bad for the children, bald and bound on wheelchairs, and their parents who looked weary and worried. I thanked God that the cyst was not cancerous. From that moment on, each time I started getting worried or exhausted, I stopped myself mid track and said a prayer of gratitude instead. It could have been worse, I thought.

In the midst of it all, I was also preparing for the birth of my third child. My in-laws were wonderful, warm people. Their kindness made the transition easier, and I would be forever grateful for that.

My sister-in-law took me shopping for baby essentials. My mother-in-law introduced me to stores like TJ Maxx and Marshalls. "You can find designer everything here for half the price," she said with a knowing smile. Being an immigrant herself, she understood the value of practicality.

She also gave me one of the most enduring lessons I've carried with me- one that many immigrants, especially those with families back home, find hard to learn. She knew, from our conversations, that I regularly sent money to my family in the Philippines.

"I understand why you do it," she said gently one afternoon as we folded baby clothes together. "I did the same for my parents. But remember- if you give away too much, you'll all end up with nothing."

Her words settled into me slowly, like a truth I didn't want to admit. At first, I brushed it off. I was raised to believe that you take care of your family, no matter what. That to say no was unkind, even dishonorable.

But over time, I began to understand what she meant- not as a warning, but as a form of protection.

That lesson came rushing back during a particularly tight season. We had just paid the mortgage, bought groceries, and covered a few unexpected bills when a message came in from home- someone needed help again. My instinct was to figure out how to make it work, even if it meant pulling from what little cushion we had. But I paused. I remembered her voice: "If you give away too much, you'll all end up with nothing."

That night, I cried in the dark, torn between guilt and reality. I wasn't used to choosing myself- or my own children. But I did. I sent what I could, and no more. It didn't feel like enough, but I reminded myself: I'm not abandoning them. I'm preserving something too. A future. Stability. The strength to keep giving, little by little, without losing myself in the process.

That decision to give less than I was asked, haunted me at first. The guilt lingered, whispering that I was failing my family. But over time, I began to see the truth in what my mother-in-law had said. Giving isn't always about the amount- it's about intention, about longevity. I realized that if I burned myself out trying to meet every need, I wouldn't be able to help anyone for long.

Eventually, I found the courage to talk to Bugsy. I told her gently but firmly, "It's your turn now. I've done what I could for so long, but I need to take care of my own growing family too." I worried how she might take it, but she understood. We talked honestly, something we hadn't done in a long time. We came to an agreement: now we take turns helping the family. The burden, once mine alone, became shared. And with that, something softened in me. I felt less alone.

My giving became more measured- but also more meaningful. I no longer gave out of guilt or obligation. I gave when I could, with a full heart, knowing I wasn't abandoning anyone- I was just finally allowing myself to breathe. I learned to trust that love doesn't always look like remittances or balikbayan boxes. Sometimes, love is setting boundaries that protect everyone in the long run. Sometimes, love is saying: "Not today, but I'm still here."

Several weeks later, I gave birth via c-section to my third child, a girl. We named her Danielle Lourdes, after my husband, Dan, and my mother, Lourdes.

She was precious; her cheeks and lips were plump and pink; I couldn't help but squeeze them. So beautiful! Her brothers came in the hospital room excited to meet her. Rence was especially excited, running/walking in with his body cast and wanting to climb in bed to get a closer look at his baby sister. Mark was right next to the bed, lovingly gazing, a proud big brother once again.

Recovering from a c-section, taking care of an infant and a two-year-old in a cast could have been more challenging, if not for the loving care and help from my oldest son and my husband. Looking back now, I don't think I could have done it without them.

A couple of months after, Dan went back to Baguio to pack up our apartment and ship our belongings to the US while I stayed behind with the children. We'd decided to make the move permanent, given Rence's care needs and the opportunities ahead. He told me that my sister and brothers helped pack up our belongings and their sadness was masked only by the relief that Rence is in recovery. My family and I didn't have our proper goodbyes. We just left, certainly not by choice but by necessity. It would be many years before I would see them again.

When Dan came back, our lives settled into a new rhythm- feeding a newborn, managing school pickups, diaper changes, cast adjustments, and midnight lullabies. It wasn't easy, but somehow, we found grace in the chaos. In the quiet hours, holding my baby girl close while her brothers played nearby, I realized that motherhood is made of moments like these-splintered days stitched together by love, fear, and unwavering hope. And though my heart had been scattered across hospital rooms and time zones, it was also fuller than ever- beating bravely in the bodies of my three beautiful children.

As we went about our new normal, Dan and I were anxious for the six-month mark to arrive. I slowly settled into life in the US. A life that included hospital visits for Rence. Six months passed and we were back in the hospital. The aspiration didn't dissuade the cyst from coming back so a few months after, Dr Gertz opened up Rence's left femur, manually sucked out the cyst, packed the bone with calcium, healthy bone chips and steroid. Each year he had to get an MRI to make sure the bone is getting denser. It was good for five years.

Then when Rence was seven years old, he had to undergo the same aspiration procedure. He was back on a body cast and was also in second grade at that time. I was initially worried that it would make him self-conscious and uncomfortable, that he would be bullied. But it was quite the opposite. He was in great spirits as ever and he found more friends, explaining to them why he was in a body cast.

Ah, the resilience of youth is something to behold...

My son Mark adjusted well. He made good grades in school and met new friends in our neighborhood. Our next-door neighbor's sons welcomed Mark with open arms. In our community, only Mark and I looked different, the only Asian. I was grateful and appreciative that our neighbors saw past the color of our skin, but it was a quiet reminder that I was adjusting to more than just a new home. I was adjusting to an entirely different world.

Sometimes, when the house was finally quiet, I would gather my children close and gently massage the pressure points on their fingers. It was something I had learned from my mother, who had once pressed the same points on mine when I was sick or anxious, whispering that it would help the pain go away. I never questioned it- it simply became truth. And now, it became ritual. My children grew so used to it that they'd climb into my lap and extend their hands without a word, trusting that I would know what to do. That small act, inherited and now passed on, became our silent language of comfort. In a world where so much felt uncertain- diagnoses, transitions, endless to-do lists - this was something I could offer: the healing power of touch, the memory of being held.

Moving abruptly to the US, I didn't know exactly what I expected, but I wasn't prepared for the loneliness of being so far from my family, my support system. I missed them terribly.

I called my mother every day, sometimes in tears. I had spent years pushing forward, always moving toward the next goal, but now, without my family nearby, I felt unmoored. "I know I have to be here, but being so far away from all of you is harder than I imagined,"

I told her over the phone, my voice breaking. "Hang in there," she said, her tone steady as always. "You've been through much worse. This too shall pass."

Even from across the ocean, she knew how to steady me, how to keep me moving forward.

I was also not prepared for the sheer abundance of choices. It was overwhelming! Malls in the Philippines back then were just as large, but here, even a single store seemed to have endless options. Walking through the aisles, I found myself hesitating, unsure of what to pick. It felt excessive, almost indulgent.

Even restaurant portions were staggering. Each time I received my food order, I wondered, how much can one person eat? The plates were bigger than my head! It brought back memories of my mother's lessons at the dinner table: "Don't waste food, but don't gorge yourself either. If you're full, stop eating. Save the rest for later."

She would remind us that there were starving children in Africa. Other times, she would remind us that gluttony was one of the seven sins. My mother, always a well of wisdom.

I never worked in my field again. To do so would have required additional U.S. college credits- time and money I simply didn't have with three children to care for, with one needing more care during the first few years of being in the US. I told myself it was the best decision for my family, and in many ways, it was. But some days, I wondered what might have been if I'd had the time, the resources, the support to continue.

I took on seasonal part time jobs when my youngest was a toddler. When all my children were in school including my youngest in pre-school, I finally had more time to have a full-time job. At that time, I was introduced to wine when I was working part time for the Country Club down the street; I started helping with the wine program. One of the members told me he was starting a wine distribution business and asked me if I could work for him. I said yes! Once again, I found myself starting over- but this time, I was armed with the confidence that no challenge was too big. If I could build a life for my family across two continents, I could certainly learn the intricacies of wine and sales.

I would often hang out in my restaurant accounts building my relationships with the buyers. In one of my big restaurant accounts, I got to talk to one of their regulars. In one of our conversations, his work in oil and gas and my background in Engineering came up. A few months later, he offered me a job that combined my engineering background and sales experience. It was a no brainer; I accepted the job. It was a whole new world that I was looking forward to learning more about and excelling in.

Through these different industries, I was able to travel the world and see some of the places that I only read in books. They have opened my eyes to new opportunities and possibilities. I often think about the people who offered me jobs, who saw in me the fire and the potential to do well, to be an asset in their companies. They have largely let me be me, which can be challenging. Not much of that feisty, confident, outspoken girl from the province has changed. Except perhaps for the scars, seen and unseen, and the lessons she has learned along the way.

Life took me in directions I never planned- across continents, through industries I never imagined, into challenges I never saw coming. I fought battles I shouldn't have had to fight, but I won them anyway. I built a life, a family, a future. And looking back now, I know one thing for sure: I was never untouchable. I was unstoppable.

Motherhood broke me open in a thousand small ways, like wood splintering under pressure. But piece by piece, through sutures and stitches, I came back together- stronger in the joints, softer in the heart.

Chapter 20: What Remains

"Loss is a kind of arrival."—Meghan O'Rourke

"May mga paang di mo maririnig, pero naroon pa rin and kanilang yapak." (There are footsteps you can no longer hear, but their tracks remain.)—Unknown

It took me 15 years to write this memoir. But the moment it truly began was a single phone call: "Dad is missing," my sister Bugsy said.

"What? How?" I answered back.

Five years earlier, I had to go back home to the Philippines because my father had a heart attack. Learning that he had a heart attack was a shock because he never had any heart issues before.

According to my mother, he was just walking down the street with one of his friends when he suddenly fell to the ground, unresponsive. He was rushed to the hospital where they were told he had a heart attack. My sister Bugsy, by now a doctor, and living in the city rushed back to our province and went straight to the provincial hospital. She found our dad being Ambu bagged by a nurse, who happened to be one of our cousins. Ambu bagging is the process of using a bag valve mask (BVM) to manually ventilate a patient. It's also known as manual resuscitator ventilation or bag mask ventilation (BMV). Even in 2005, the provincial hospital didn't have mechanical ventilators, so it had to be done manually. My sister immediately had our father transported by ambulance to the city hospital. She later told me that it was the longest ride of her life.

I can still remember the shock I felt when I opened the door to his hospital room. Two orderlies were helping him change his diaper, and as he looked up and caught my eyes, I saw the look of helplessness and confusion in his eyes, like he didn't recognize me. The father I knew wasn't in that body. I had to quickly turn around and leave the room before he could see me cry.

Nothing ever prepares you for the moment you realize that the man you always looked up to, the strong, resilient man, can't even help himself. The look I saw in his eyes is still with me to this day.

The doctor informed us the following day that he had the early onset of dementia. They explained that it is because it took the physicians almost thirty minutes to revive him in the ER. Thirty minutes without oxygen. That's what the doctors told us. That's what stole him from us- slowly, then permanently.

It resulted in hypoxic encephalopathy, a condition where the brain is deprived of oxygen. This condition can significantly increase the risk of developing dementia, particularly in severe cases, as it can cause widespread brain damage that impacts cognitive function and memory, leading to symptoms similar to dementia.

The room fell silent as the doctor's words settled over us like a heavy fog. Dementia. The reality of it pressed down on our chests, suffocating. My mother slowly lowered herself into a chair, her face unreadable, but I saw it- the fear, the uncertainty.

Jun, steady as always, simply said, "We'll figure it out." Chris, the youngest, had no words- just silent tears slipping down his face. Bugsy, ever the doctor, tried to make sense of it for us, but even she couldn't soften the blow.

She was, in many ways, a mirror of our mother's gentler strength-steadfast, nurturing, quietly powerful. The two of them shared an unspoken language, a way of understanding people's hearts without needing too many words. Bugsy had inherited that grace, and used it to hold us together when distance, pride, or pain might have pulled us apart. If I was the storm, she was the shelter. If I was the bold declaration, she was the quiet through-line that made it all make sense.

But even the strongest threads are tested. Not long after I moved to the US, my mother retired from teaching and made a decision that stunned us all. Without consulting any of us, she took out her retirement in a lump sum and invested it in a construction business owned by one of her brothers and a cousin. Within a year, the company went bust- and with it, everything she had saved.

I was livid. Not just because of the money, but because she hadn't told us. Because she had trusted so blindly. Because she, the woman who had taught us to be cautious and wise, had been reckless with her own future. I couldn't even speak to her. The words wouldn't come without fire, and I knew they would only burn.

So, Bugsy stepped in.

She did what she always did. She sat beside my mother, listened, comforted. She called me not to excuse the decision, but to remind me of the whole story, the weight of my mother's intentions, the shame she was already carrying. "She thought she was helping," Bugsy said gently. "She thought she could leave something more behind."

And in that moment, I didn't soften- not entirely- but I began to understand. Bugsy, like my mother, didn't ask me to let go of my anger. She just held it until I was ready to put it down. Bugsy stood in the wreckage of that silence, holding the threads that bound us, reminding us- me especially- that love, though bruised, was still there, waiting to be mended.

Looking back, I realize that moment wasn't just about money or misjudgment. It was about how deeply we carry our hopes- for safety, for dignity, for something to show for a life of sacrifice. My mother risked it all for a dream of security. I responded with silence because I didn't know how to grieve that kind of loss. But Bugsy- Bugsy reminded me that love isn't measured by flawless choices, but by the courage to stay in the conversation. And that grace, that capacity to return to each other even when we're hurt, is its own kind of inheritance.

The doctor explained what lay ahead: moments of clarity that would come and go, memories slipping through his fingers like sand, until eventually, there would be more darkness than light.

I turned to my father, asleep in his hospital bed. Did he know what was happening? Did he understand what he was losing?

And more importantly, what had caused his heart attack? He never had any known heart issues.

Our mother speculated much later that it might have been due to stress. He had been on his way to meet with his grassroots group- the same one that had fought so hard for agricultural land rights. Someone, or perhaps several people in power, were once again trying to reverse the ruling, to steal back the land the government had initially seized through eminent domain. It was a sobering realization: the fight never really ends. And once again, my mother was right- stress can kill.

Then, my mother spoke, quiet but firm. "We'll just have to do what we always do. Keep going."

Her voice was steady, but her eyes held an uncertainty I had never seen before.

It was decided that Mom and Dad would live at my sister's house in the province, with my siblings helping whenever they could. Our mother's large extended family would also support her as she became our father's caretaker. I would continue sending financial assistance from the US.

Months earlier, before my father's heart attack, I had tried to bring my mother to visit me and my family in the US. I was told I needed to write her a formal letter of petition, expressing my wish for her to visit. Armed with that letter, she traveled to Manila and applied at the US embassy. She was denied a visitor's visa.

"Why?" my mother asked.

"Because you answered yes to the question: are you being petitioned?"

the consul replied.

"That's because I have a letter of petition from my daughter to visit her," my mother explained.

"No- the question was asking if you are being petitioned to become a US citizen," the consul retorted.

"Your question was incomplete. If it were phrased the way you just said it, I would have answered no," my mother persisted.

"Come back in six months and reapply. You'll start fresh with the questionnaire," the consul told her.

She did. Six months later, she traveled by bus to Manila again, only to be denied once more-this time still based on her earlier answer to an unclear question.

"I felt like a criminal!" she told me over the phone, distraught. She had endured long hours of travel, twice, only to be humiliated and dismissed. We were all frustrated. I felt helpless, angry, and deeply sorry for her.

We decided to wait a couple of years before she would try again.

But before that could happen, Dad had the heart attack.

I had a young family to take care of, so I returned to the US knowing that I am leaving behind my mother to take care of a loved one, like she always did. "God," I thought, "will her sacrifice ever end?"

257

"Did you hear what I just said? Dad has gone missing!" My sister's voice jarred me back to the present.

She told me that dad was able to unlock the house from the inside and wandered off. He has not returned overnight. She told me that the whole town was looking for him.

My sister's house in the province was set far back from the main road and surrounded by trees and vegetation. It wasn't isolated for a normal human being to navigate, but one with dementia can get easily turned around and get lost. It was also in the middle of the summer so he could have also been easily exhausted.

"How long has dad been gone?" I asked.

Seven days now, my sister said. I asked why they didn't inform me earlier.

"We were holding hope that we find him quickly," she quietly said.

I told her I'm booking a flight and coming home. She told me to hold off for a day. I said "Ok. Let's give it another day," then hung up, hoping to God he was okay.

I couldn't wait; I booked my flight. I called my sister to tell her.

"That's good then. I'm sure mom will appreciate that," she said.

I was halfway through packing when the phone rang. My sister's voice was barely a whisper.

"They found Dad. He's gone."

The words didn't register at first. Then, like a dam breaking, the weight of them crashed over me. My knees buckled, and I collapsed onto the floor, sobbing.

My children rushed in, startled by my grief. I forced myself to find the words- "Lolo is gone"-but they were too young to fully understand. Their concern was for me, not for the grandfather they barely knew.

Regret tightened around my throat. I had let time slip away, let distance widen the gap between us. Now, that gap was permanent. Sadness turned into guilt, heavy and unforgiving.

I arrived at midnight in Manila. As I made my way out of the terminal, I couldn't help but notice the big balikbayan (going home) boxes that other passengers were schlepping as pasalubong (gifts) for their Filipino families. I imagined their happy reunions, and it made me sadder knowing why I was there.

Outside the terminal, the hot humid air was stifling adding to the discomfort I was already feeling. The place was crowded and noisy as I strained to find my brother in the crowd. We finally found each other- we hugged and cried. We quickly made our way out to meet our cousin who would take turns driving with my brother the long ride home.

We made small talk during the drive to help keep whoever was driving awake. Mostly, I was lost in thought. I was exhausted. As the sun slowly rose in the horizon and I can see my old country in the daylight, I was amazed at how much have changed and how much remained the same.

The mountains were still beautiful, green, and lush. The winding roads that made traveling fun were still, well, winding. The highways were wider but still congested with traffic. The towns and cities we passed by had taller buildings, and more people. We stopped at one of the roadside restaurants to eat, they were bigger yet still felt packed. Everybody seemed to be going everywhere.

The familiar feeling of home started to fill the air as the mountains got higher and the roads became windier. The realization of why I was there got heavier. When we finally reached my sister's house, I lost it. My mother, looking sad and exhausted, met me halfway on the graveled drive that led to my sister's house. There was nothing to say, we just hugged and cried.

In my province, the vigil for the dead is at the immediate family's residence. After a day or two, the vigil moves to another relatives' house before finally getting buried at a family cemetery. Traditionally, the dead person's stature in the community would dictate the number of days a vigil should be held; 3 days is the minimum and up to 5 days, sometimes 7 days if the dead person is rich and of very high stature. In my father's case, five days.

So, when I arrived, my father's casket was in my sister's living room the first two days of vigil.

It was a closed casket. My father was lost for seven days. He couldn't find his way home due to his dementia. It was a hot summer, so the weather and nature took what they take, and what's left was what's in the casket. One of my cousins asked if I wanted to see a picture of how my father was found. I declined to see it.

As I mingled with those who came to pay their respects at my father's wake, I found myself drifting between the familiar and the unfamiliar faces from long ago, softened by time, and strangers who somehow still knew who I was. There was comfort in the reconnection, even in the shadow of grief. Each handshake and hug felt like a thread tying me to a life once lived.

"Hi, I'm Jane. I'm not sure if you remember me," I said, offering a warm smile to someone whose face I vaguely recognized, though his name escaped me.

"Oh yeah, you're the one who got pregnant in high school!"

I froze. My smile faltered for a split second- but years of practiced composure kicked in.

"Yes, that would be me," I replied with a laugh that tried too hard to be light, then quickly excused myself.

As I walked away, my face burned. My palms were damp. The air around me suddenly felt too thick, the room too small. It hit me then, like a low blow to the gut- I will always be that girl to some people. No matter what I've done since. No matter how far I've come. That single chapter in my life has left an ink stain that some still choose to see first.

And that's a bitter pill to swallow. A pill coated in shame, even now, even after all this time.

Yes, there are those who reach out to say they're proud of what I've made of my life. They tell me I'm strong, that I've overcome so much. And I am grateful- truly- that some people see beyond the story they thought they knew.

But the sting of stigma, when flung so casually, so publicly, can still knock the wind out of me. It reminded me that for some, growth will always be secondary to gossip.

I've learned to live with it, the whispers and the side glances, the way my story gets reduced to a footnote in someone else's memory. I've learned to hold my head high. I've stitched myself back together more times than I can count.

Still, I wonder- how long do the bumps on the road stay? Do they eventually smooth out, or do we simply learn to drive better, to steer without flinching?

The following day, my father's casket was moved to the next town over, to the house of one of my aunts. There, my siblings and I rehearsed the song we wanted to sing for our father's funeral the next day. We were emotionally exhausted, but we knew we had to push through.

It was the last vigil that night, and we had an Irish wake. I do not recall the stories told, but we laughed a lot, cried laughing sometimes. We all knew what was coming, but somehow, being around the people who loved my father made it okay to laugh, to smile, to have fun, to tell stories, in celebration of his life. It was early the following morning when the last story was told.

I didn't cry a lot during the vigil, even when my father's casket was entombed. I think in a way I saw it as the end of his suffering, as well as my mother's. For five years, she took care of him, even when he became mean to her and everyone around him. His moments of lucidity became shorter and shorter, but my mother loved him through it all.

During my plane ride back to the US, I thought of all the things that my father and I left unsaid. We used to talk a lot about what I wanted to be when I grew up. After I got pregnant at 16, we talked so little. He stopped dreaming my dreams. And I let him. Now, there was only silence.

One of my biggest regrets is that he never met his granddaughter, my youngest. She was born in the US, but they couldn't get a visitor's visa. And now, it's too late. He will never meet her- the smart, gifted, spunky, athletic girl she's become. She's a strong swimmer, like he was, competing at the regional level before high school. She's also a dancer, just like he was, and went on to study at an art high school and university. There are so many things I wish he could have shared with his granddaughter and grandsons, moments they'll never know.

I thought about the last time I heard his voice. I tried to remember what he said, how he said it, whether he smiled. But the memory was slippery. I hated that. I hated that grief felt like forgetting.

There are things my father never said- truths knotted in history, pride, and pain. And yet, he left behind a language all his own. Not of words, but of gestures: the way he stood a little straighter when others tried to take what was his, the way he labored over land not to own it, but to feel rooted. The house we never knew became a door, not just into his past, but into mine. Into ours. In the end, he gave me no riches, no roadmap- only the soft weight of resilience pressed into my bones. And maybe that is the truest inheritance: to carry someone forward, not just in memory, but in the way you walk through the world.

Somewhere over the Pacific, I let the tears come. Not loud sobs, just quiet weeping- the kind that lives in the throat and behind the eyes. The kind only the sky can hold.

On that plane ride, my book began forming in my mind. I tried writing, but each time, the emotions overwhelmed me. I'd scribble a few thoughts, misplace them, start again, and stop. For years, my book existed only in my mind. In the book are some of the conversations I should have had with my father. I would have told him I was sorry I disappointed him, and he would tell me, it was okay. I would tell him that I made something of myself, despite everything. He would tell me; he was proud of me.

In time, I also came to understand that my personal story was not just my own- it was intertwined with larger forces. Growing up under Martial Law, witnessing People Power, and later navigating systems shaped by patriarchy and colonial hangovers, I learned that survival, especially for women like me, was an act of quiet rebellion. I began to see how our stories- our pain, our resilience- were political. I could no longer look at injustice, at inequity, at the silencing of voices like my mother's and mine, without feeling compelled to think, to speak, to act, to lead.

I used to think that politics was something distant, something reserved for men in suits or generals in fatigues. But the older I got, the more I understood that politics was personal. It was in the long bus rides my mother took to the U.S. embassy only to be met with humiliation. It was in the missing persons during Martial Law, in the charred body of my friend's sister, in the way girls like me were judged for our mistakes but rarely offered grace. I began to see how power shaped our everyday lives- who had it, who abused it, who paid the price. And in those quiet awakenings, a different kind of fire took root in me.

Over the years, I saw women rise. Not because the world made space for them, but because they carved space out with their bare hands. My mother, who bore so much and still stood with dignity. My sister Bugsy, through her calm and open heart, managed to hold us together across oceans and continents. The nuns and teachers who shielded us during the chaos. The women in government, in protest lines, in community halls- each one claiming her voice in a world that often tried to silence her. Their courage made mine possible. And now, as I tell this story- my story- I realize that I, too, have stepped into a kind of power. Not the kind that rules countries, but the kind that refuses to stay quiet. The kind that remembers, names, and builds. The kind that writes it all down, so the next girl knows she's not alone.

Mom at 78, still tending to nature, her favorite pastime

Indeed, the journey to my dreams was circuitous, full of twists and unexpected turns. Along the way, I discarded some childhood dreams and shaped new ones. The road was fraught with heartache and doubt, but it also offered moments of unexpected joy and love.

Life continued to unfold in ways I never anticipated. The man who once rescued me, the father of my children, became a part of my past. But I will always be grateful for the life we built and the family we created. Though our paths diverged, I carry only gratitude- only appreciation for the role he played in my story. And now, with a heart-fully open and unguarded-, to love once more, I walk forward with the person I believe I will spend the rest of my life with.

Along the way, I found my voice- as a woman, a mother, and a Filipina navigating life between two cultures.

But that voice wasn't born in comfort- it was stirred awake in silence, in fear, in the slow unlearning of everything I had once accepted as normal. In the chapter Shadows and Sunrises, I wrote about the early days of Martial Law, the curfews, the whispers, and the weight of things unspoken. That chapter didn't just mark a political regime- it marked the moment I first began to question systems, power, and truth. I came to understand that politics isn't just in laws or elections. It's in who gets to speak and who is silenced. Who gets to dream freely, and who is punished for daring. That early awareness planted the seed for the voice I carry now- one that names what hurts, but also what heals.

I learned that strength doesn't always look like loud proclamations; sometimes it's quiet persistence, sometimes it's showing up again and again. In boardrooms and community halls, I began to see how rare and vital it is for women of all color to hold power and use it to uplift others. I believe in the power of women's leadership not just because I lived it. My mother's quiet courage, my sister's intellect, and my own journey from shame to self-respect have shown me that when women rise, families rise, communities rise.

There were days when the weight of it all felt unbearable- when I questioned whether I was strong enough, smart enough, or simply lucky enough to rise above my circumstances. But there was a fire inside me that no hardship could extinguish, a faith that anchored me through every storm. It was my mother's voice reminding me to pray, to trust, to believe in my ability to overcome.

For years, I carried the weight of responsibility for my family's needs back home, often stretching myself thin. There were times I struggled with guilt- guilt for not doing more, for choosing myself, for setting limits. But since I have opened up to my sister and we've taken turns supporting our family, it's no longer a burden carried alone, but a shared act of love. That simple shift brought not only relief, but healing. We had each found our way to honor our roles, not out of obligation, but out of balance, compassion, and growth. With that, we have become closer than ever.

There are stories I carry that are still unfolding- threads that tug at me quietly, in moments of stillness.

My youngest brother Chris is one of them.

He loved music! He was drawn to the hum of strings and the rhythm of melody. The guitar was his voice, and on stage, he came alive- his smile wide, his joy uncontained. In another life, I think he would have made music his world, formed a band, toured city to city, left a trail of chords in his wake. But in this life, he chose the steadier path of engineering. A practical choice, maybe even a selfless one. One no one questioned, not even me.

Sometimes I wish I had asked more questions- about his dreams, about what he wanted outside of what was expected. But I was overwhelmed, too wrapped in motherhood and survival and making things right. He was only seven years younger than me, but those years pulled us in different directions, like branches from the same tree reaching toward separate skies.

We have spoken a lot more about things that matter, now that we are older and wiser, but I still hold him in my thoughts the way I hold so many others- not just for who he is, but for what might have been. The things we don't say to those we love can sometimes echo the loudest. And maybe part of growing older is learning how to live with the echoes.

I've spent much of my life straddling two worlds- belonging everywhere and nowhere all at once. I was shaped by a homeland that taught me resilience and by an adopted land that challenged me to reclaim my voice. The path has not been easy, but it has been mine.

It is a strange kind of peace to finally feel comfortable in my own skin- especially in a country whose history is stained with centuries of discrimination and violence against people of color. Sometimes, when someone says, "Your skin is beautiful- it's golden," I pause. I feel both seen and unsettled. Have we, as a society, been so shaped by centuries of prejudice that something as innocent as skin tone became a scapegoat for fear, bias, even violence? If so, are we destined to repeat the cycles of colorism and racism again and again? Still, I remain hopeful. I believe in our capacity for reflection, for growth, for healing. I believe our innate goodness can prevail.

Somewhere along the way, I stopped seeing my scars as proof of what broke me and started seeing them as the stitches that held me together. Life cut deep- but it also mended. And every thread, every suture, told a story of a woman who chose to rise, again and again. Not untouched but transformed.

Life didn't turn out how I planned at 16. It turned out better, in ways I could never have imagined. And as I reflect on this journey, I can't help but think of my children.

To my children: this story is yours as much as it is mine. You are the continuation of all the stories I carry- the ones I lived, the ones I inherited, the ones I fought to rewrite. May you walk forward knowing where you come from and may that knowing strengthen your stride.

My firstborn, my greatest gift, who put me on the straight and narrow and showed me how strong a person I could be. Because of you, I found the strength to keep forging ahead, a strength that made it possible for me to have two more beautiful children. You have all shaped me into the person I am today- a proud mother. I rose so you can rise higher. More importantly, I want you to know that life's beauty often lies in its unpredictability. That even in the noise and confusion, the drudgery and broken dreams, there is still so much to be grateful for.

So may you rise with courage, love with your whole heart, and always believe that something beautiful can come from even the most uncertain path.

"And whatever your labors and aspirations, in the noisy confusion of life, keep peace with your soul. With all its sham, drudgery and broken dreams, it is still a beautiful world."
  —Desiderata

Epilogue: The Gift of October

"The power is in the telling, not the approval."
  -The author

There are stories we inherit, and there are stories we choose to carry forward.

For a long time, I didn't know the difference. Like my father, who carried his own untold stories, I lived in the spaces between expectation and survival, holding silences that weren't mine alone. But in writing this, I've come to understand that healing doesn't come from forgetting- it comes from remembering with intention.

I didn't set out to be brave. I simply chose not to disappear. Again, and again.

What began as a chronicle of pain became something else entirely. A record of resilience. A map of memory. A testament to my mother's fierce, unconditional love- and her unconventional lessons that stitched me back together. A quiet homage to the skin I once wanted to shed, and eventually learned to live in. A love letter to the people and places that shaped me, broke me, and helped me gather the pieces again.

271

I offer this story not as a conclusion, but as an opening- for connection, for conversation, for anyone who has ever stood at the edge of their own shadows and wondered if light would find them again.

It will.

And when it does, may you stand in it fully- unhidden, unbroken, unstoppable, and beautifully seen. And ready to uncover the deeper purpose only pain and persistence can reveal.

In the end, what remains isn't just memory- it's the quiet strength of those who stayed.

Just as my mother always said, "We'll do what we always do. Keep Going."

And so I did.

And so I will.

About the Author

Sheilah Jane was born in the Philippines and now calls the U.S. home. She's a certified yoga instructor and co-founder of Sempre Avanti Imports, where she travels to meet and break bread with families before importing their wines—a testament to her deep belief in connection and care.

With a degree in engineering and a life forged by resilience, she writes for the girls who carry secrets, the women who rise from them, and anyone learning to begin again. Shadows and Sunrises is her debut memoir.

You can connect with me on:
🌐 https://sheilahjane.com

Subscribe to my newsletter:

✉ http://subscribepage.io/Shadows_and_Sunrises